Death Cave
By
Zeke Crandall

About this book

This book is published by Zeke Crandall LLC., 6210 West Shaw Butte Drive, Glendale, 85304

All rights to this book in any form are strictly prohibited unless authorized by the author, with all copyrights reserved.

The ISBN number is 978-0-9773784-9-4 the book's copyright number through the United States Library of Congress is TXu1-816-579; June 25, 2012

Soft bound signed copies of the Death Cave Man are available for sale at discounted internet pricing on our website, www.arizonatales.com or by email, my email address is zekecrandall46@hotmail.com.

Other books from this author can be found on Amazon, (Createspace.com) and EBay. All books are signed by the author. The author can also be reached on cell phone number 602 399-1811

Thank you,
Zeke Crandall

Preface

While living in Prescott three days a week with my late mother, working as her caregiver, the author spent quite a bit of time at the Sharlot Hall Museum Archives building doing research for my Canyon Diablo book.

In the process of doing research on Canyon Diablo, the author came across so much information regarding another town that was three miles south of Canyon Diablo, the Atlantic & Pacific railroad town that I was able to write a complete story of the town of Two Guns, along with the history of the area including a little about Canyon Diablo.

The most amazing story surfaced as I researched for these two book, a cave some three miles long and with a large enough entrance that a man on horse could enter, then once inside, there were two caverns large enough each to hold a small herd of horses.

Then as the author mentioned this cave to several friends, one of them Jeff Dunn, told me that he had been in the cave on many occasions. He told me that there was no sign of any life form, ever being in the cave. He went on to say that he in fact spent the night in the cave on a couple of occasions. He said it is 60 degrees in the cave all year round. He was even able to light a campfire.

The author spoke to a Navajo Medicine man, who has a shop in downtown Prescott, who told me that he had never heard of the cave but said that if there is no life form in the cave, not an animal dropping or anything, that it was probably a burial a Native American burial site.

When the author told the medicine man about the death of 54 Apaches that were part of a raiding party that attacked several nearby Navajo villages and were killed in the cave, he told me that my fears about entering the cave were justified. He said there is no doubt that an Apache Shaman left a spirit guide to guard the cave.

When this author told the medicine man that he had weird feelings about the cave, the medicine man told the author that by all means that the author should not go in the cave. He said other folks can go in and not have a problem but if the evil spirit that dwells in the cave decides to hook on to anyone of them, that they will have a life of bad luck.

When I told him about all of the owners' bad luck he just looked at me and said that he was not surprised but it would be wise for me not to enter the cave.

Below is a photo of the entrance of the Death Cave that was taken by the author's friend Jeff Dunn.

Chapter One

The history of man in the area around the ghost towns of Canyon Diablo and Two Guns located in Northern Arizona dates back to the Dawn of Man. The first Native American inhabitants were followed by the Basket Makers, then Pueblo periods one and two. These Anasazi and Sinagua people built dwellings in the cliffs of the canyon. The greatest density of the inhabitants was between 700 and 1600 A.D., with the greatest Native American population from 1050 to 1300, when the land on the Coconino Plateau was made fertile by the disintegration of the volcanic fields from the San Francisco Peaks to the west.

Even before man was known to live in this area, some 22,000 years ago, a giant nickel-iron meteor weighing several million tons and traveling at a speed of 133,000 miles per hour, plunged into the earth creating a huge crater just east of the two towns, that lie on the north and south side, respectfully of Interstate 40, thirty miles west of Flagstaff and thirty miles east of Winslow, destroyed all life for a one hundred mile radius. The meteor is estimated to have been on 81 feet in diameter and the crater it left after impact is nearly a mile in diameter and 600 feet deep. Some prehistoric peoples left ruins within the rim of the crater, indicating they found it a suitable place to live.

The Meteor Crater wasn't considered to have been caused by a meteorite until 1886, when sheepherders found pieces of meteorites near Canyon Diablo. In 1891, a leading geologist, G.K. Gilbert, declared that the crater had not been made by a meteor. It wasn't until 1903 when Dr. Daniel Barringer, a mining engineer, convinced that a large metallic meteor had created the crater, began drilling at the site, but he was unsuccessful in mining the mineral ore. His project to locate the main mass of the meteorite was abandoned in 1929 after drilling to a depth of nearly 1400 feet on the southeastern slope of the crater. Modern technology reveals that about 80% of the meteorite had been vaporized on impact and that only about 10% of it still lies beneath the south rim.

The first known Europeans to see Canyon Diablo were Spaniards from part of Coronado's expedition into New Mexico in 1540-1542. They were let by Captain Don Garcia E. Cardenas, and were sent by Coronado from the Hopi villages to find the Grand Canyon on the Colorado River. They crossed the canyon where it enters the Little Colorado River.

On the next page is a railroad postcard of the Meteor Crater owned by the author, circa 1910

Over the next 300 years, countless explorers, settlers, traders and treasure seekers, trying to establish a direct route to the beautiful San Francisco Peaks on the western horizon and from there to the Pacific Ocean, were confronted with the 300-foot chasm of Canyon Diablo, and were forced to make a detour of some 25 miles either north or south in order to proceed across the Little Colorado River.

Below is a photo of Two Guns taken recently by Jeff Dunn looking down into Canyon Diablo near Two Guns.

Chapter Two

In this chapter the author would like to continue with the history of the area, the founding people of the Little Colorado River basin and Canyon Diablo itself because it is the basis of this story. Across the broad, calm face of Northern Arizona winds the thin, red scar of a river. A river so alive and unstable, turbulent and temperamental is a vicious but vital, unique river. At times you could cross it and never know it existed. During the summer months it can be just a trickle of rust colored water running through it and even dry in some places. In fact it is not really dry. The river actually flows underground in those places that appear dry. If one looks closely, the river streambed can be a hundred yards wide in places that gives away its potential size. It is a small river, as rivers go. But the Little Colorado raises a lot of hell, during the months of April, May and June, on its short journey from the high mountains of the Northeastern Arizona, Mogollon Rim country to the big Colorado River that lies a hundred miles to the East.

In winter, the snow lies heavy over the jagged peaks of the White Mountains. The April sun begins to warm the browses to greenness and the first shimmering beads seep from the melting snow banks.

Thousands of small creeks and rivulets, that feed's the Little Colorado gather intensity as they tumble downward. Lower down the mountain, a clear, gentle trout stream has formed, sparkling in the spring air. Past Greer, the river runs into a series of idyllic lakes, a man-made paradise for fishermen and boaters. Now the river, tamed at intervals by the dams and reservoirs that were built by the Mormon settlers that irrigate the arid land, and flow through peaceful orchards, small farms and pastures that provide drinking water for their cattle, horses and their other farm animals.

The Little Colorado River gives life to one Mormon settlement after another: including the towns of Greer, Eager, St Johns, Hunt, Woodruff, Joseph City, North of St Johns, the river grows with tributaries as violent and unstable as the creeks Carrizo, Zuni, Puerco, Leroux, Cottonwood, and the Manila. At that point the Little Colorado River runs free again, shed of its dams, and ditches, running loose through the cattle and sheep country of Northern Arizona. The Painted Desert stretches to meet the horizon on the north; the Mogollon Rim protrudes from the south. Here at this point the river is most fickled and ruthless, turbid with muddy debris and playing possum.

In seasons plagued by drought, the river bed is bone-dry. After a sudden desert storm of heavy run-off from melting snow, the river lashes furiously through its banks. Most of the year, it slithers like a sidewinder along her course through the canyons, after passing Winslow, it changes, as if the river knew the end would come soon. Silently the river flows through timeless Indian country, dwarfed by the great sky, endless earth, and steep cliffs on both sides of the river, at last entering into the area held sacred by the Navajo for centuries. Just below Cameron it begins the tortuous descent through sheer canyon walls to eventually join forces with the Colorado River, before they cut through the bottom of the Grand Canyon.

The Little Colorado River, *"the old-timers used to say,"* is bounded on the North by Wolf Trading Post and on the south by Phelps Dodge Corporation copper mines. Those early day miners, cowpunchers, railroaders, farmers, teamsters, sheep herders, outlaws, saloon keepers, cavalry men and lumberjacks knew the river. All of them, who had ever crossed the arid grasslands of Northern Arizona by horse, wagon or on foot knew the Little Colorado River. They forded the river at the known crossings, bogged down in the treacherous quicksand, drank and watered their stock from the thick red stream, and fled from her unpredictable flash floods. They all knew that the river was the pulsing main artery of a country so vast and wide and unsettled that it would be remembered always as one of America's last frontier.

The mighty Mississippi, rolling with the slow-moving power, is America's, *"Old Man River."* The Colorado River, also a river of extreme value to the southwest that it supplies most of its water, cuts a grand swath through the Southwest with queenly authority from its beginning in Colorado dividing California from Arizona, and then running through Mexico to the Gulf of California. But the Little Colorado is a real harlot; it is young, reckless, tempestuous, rushing with abandon across the open country, and when the spree is over, lying low, spent and ugly, on the hot, red sand. With the next downpour, it is rejuvenated, roaring and raucous, surging and foaming in desperation over the barren land. Men have loved the river in spite of its faults, because they have needed it at one time or another.

Other men who knew her had other names for her, in *"Legend of the Chiquito Colorado,"* poet Milo Willbank of Eager, Arizona says;

> *"The Little Colorado, or Colorado Chiquito, was called Tol-Chaco by*

the Navajo Indians, meaning red or bloody water. The explorer Coronado called it Rio de Lino, or Flax River because of the wild flax that grew along its banks. It was first called Colorado, also meaning red, in by the explorer Onate. But to those who live in its arid basin, it is their life stream, without which they could not live in this, the country they love. So to each of them, it is not just a river, but the river of life: a stream of moods and passions rising in the White Mountains from clear springs."

High on the eastern slopes of Mount Baldy in the White Mountains, towering 11,470 feet above sea level, are the headwaters of the Little Colorado River. Driving east from the town of McNary, a lumbering town on Arizona State Highway 73, you turn off at the Big Lake sign and drive through rolling, grassy foothills at the base of the forested mountains. This is in the heart of Apache country, the finest cattle country in all of Arizona. In the fall, Apache cowboys and their dogs drive the sleek Herefords, along the road and up to the sale ring at Sheep Springs. Cattle buyers and on-lookers eat a hearty meal cooked out in the open, of barbecued beef, beans, coleslaw and steaming hot coffee, while the hoarse auctioneer takes a break.

At Sheep Crossing, on the Big Lake road, the big sheep outfits make their camps in summer. Basque herders, with Australian shepherd dogs herd sheep all day to the sound of tinkling bells and wind rustled pine branches. At night the aroma of lamb stew cooked with vegetables and hot bread from Dutch ovens, with the help of a breezes floats through the nearby forests. There is Bill Sterin, the cook drinking coffee and telling campfire stories. After breakfast, the burros are packed, the diamond hitches thrown and Sterin moves on to the next camp, while the sheep graze slowly toward their summer ranges near Springerville.

Below is a photo of the headwaters of the Little Colorado River at Sheep Crossing north of Springerville, Arizona, that was found on the Hiking.com website and used with their permission.

The air at Sheep Crossing is thin and clean, fragrant with pine and the scent of fresh running water. A sign is posted on the fence telling folks that the headwaters of the Little Colorado River are seven miles upstream. Fishermen move silently up and down the stream, fly-casting for trout. The path crosses a stile and follows the river upstream.

In late summer, the Little Colorado River runs fast and deep, swelled with the runoff of recent rains. It flows through a grassy valley where the smell of cows lingers along the banks. Pussy willows and poplar trees flash their leaves in the sun. After a mile or so, the gorge narrows and the river begin to run down a steeper grade. Another few miles and the path open suddenly a wide green meadow where a vacant cabin of a homestead stands alone.

On the other side of a bog, the real accent begins. The path narrows. Underbrush, boulders and fallen logs block its path. Wild berries grow along the banks. The river rumbles over a rocky bed and the sunlight scarcely filters through the tall ponderosa pines, along with blue spruce, white fir and aspen trees. Here and there on the soft sponge of the forest floor are deer prints. Higher and steeper and less distinct the path grows. Creeks run from every side into the stream, now only three of four feet across.

In the damp, green forest, the lumbering elk bugles on frosty fall nights, the wild turkey, black bear, squirrels, skunks, porcupines, cougars, bobcats, foxes, deer, wolves and even jaguars roam. The brazen blue jay screams his warning through the tall pines. There in the White Mountains of Northeastern Arizona, the Little Colorado begins her journey of hundreds of miles across the face of Northeastern Arizona to her final destination the Big Colorado River.

Not far downstream from Sheep Crossing, just below the east and, west forks of the Little Colorado, at an elevation of 8,560 feet above sea level is the mountain village of Greer. According to founding father A.V. Greer, a Mormon settler from Texas, Greer was originally called Lee Valley, after a pioneer family who saw potential in the rich mountain dirt, native grass, abundant fish and game. Because of the Little Colorado River's permanent water supply, small scale farming of oats, barley, and rye is carried on, as well as summer cutting of timothy, native hay and meadow grass for the livestock.

Although the population of Greer rarely climbs over one hundred and seventy-five, in summer there are often as many as 5,000 people in the area, there to fish, hunt, camp and some just getting away from the heat in the Valley of the Sun, some two hundred miles to the southwest. Greer has several lodges, along with several church and youth camps.

Paralleling state highway 73, the violent, at times, the young river flows from Greer into Round Valley. This wide and lovely valley 7,000 feet high, bordered on the south by timbered mountains, considered *"chinde,"* or a place of evil spirits, by the Navajo, who lived there when the first white settlers arrived. Round Valley is dissected by the Little Colorado River, which is said to have marked a boundary line between the White Mountain Apaches and the Navajo, both predominantly farmers, who shared its waters and was considered no-mans land.

In 1865, a Union scout named Tony Long passed through Round Valley in his search for a wagon load full of California gold bound for Confederate troops. Long returned again after the Civil War, this time while under contract as a freighter, he carried corn from Pueblo, Colorado in route to the Cavalry outpost at Fort Apache, in the company of fellow freighters W.R. Milligan, Marian Clark, Johnny McCullough, Dionicio Elalio, Juan Baca and Gabriel Silva. Struck once more by the potential of the fertile valley, Long and his partners built a house known as Milligan's Fort and began small scale farming. At that time Round Valley was known by its Spanish name, Valle Redondo.

Not until 1877 did the permanent settlement of Round Valley begin to arrive, with the first wagon train of determined and courageous Mormon families led by A.V. Greer and Harris Phelps, who brought their wagons, household goods and families from Texas. A year later, the first Utah Mormon pioneers arrived, establishing the First Ward, calling it the Little Colorado Stake. With the coming of the Mormons, the wild and unruly river, like a wild unbroken horse, slowly and painstakingly began to be broken. Hearty, resourceful and persevering, other pioneers such as the Holdens, Eagars, Crosbys, Willbanks and the Udall families built permanent homes, raised children, dug ditches and canals and built the dams that were necessary to irrigate their farms, gardens and orchards.

The peaceful village of Eager, named after the three Eagar brothers who came in 1878, has remained predominantly Mormon, the neighboring town of Springerville, became one of the wildest and lawless towns the West has ever seen. Named after Harry Springer, an

Albuquerque merchant, who had a branch there in the early days, Springerville was, for a time, a favorite town of all the renegade horse thieves, cattle rustlers and fugitives from the law, who came from the whole Southwest.

The draw for this lawless element was the fact that the capital of Arizona and the capital of Yavapai County was in Prescott, some three hundred miles away to the west, and so it was pretty much free from any lawmen other than a few local constables. It was a great place for this bad element to hide.

After the widely publicized Earp-Clanton shootout at the O.K. Corral in Tombstone on October 26, 1881, what was left of the notorious Clanton gang came to the White Mountain Area, where again lawmen were only conspicuous by their absence. Old man Clanton, along with his sons Ike, Phin and Leonard claimed a homestead on Coyote Creek east of Springerville. In the relative safety of their own ranch, they continued the pursuits for which their previous experience had prepared them, trading horses and cattle of questionable brands and generally stirring up trouble wherever they went.

In addition to the Clanton's, a group of men of similar temperament, occupation and reputation moved into the area, known as the

Smith Gang. By the early 1882 with the completion of the Canyon Diablo train bridge by the railroad, which ended the mad rush to the lawless town of the same name, some of the toughest outlaws ever seen in the west drifted east to the last frontier, the Springerville area.

After robbing banks and stages in Arizona's booming mining towns around Tombstone, they would ride by night to their hideouts in the Springerville area. Men of the Snyder Gang started a gun battle among themselves and before the day was over, nine of them were killed, conveniently on the hill behind the Eagar cemetery.

The Westbrook brothers, a gang from Colorado, were unscrupulous land jumpers and outlaws, who murdered James Hale, a local citizen, in the streets of Springerville in 1887. When questioned about the reasoning behind the murder of an innocent citizen, they stated that;

"They simply wanted to see if a bullet would go through a Mormon."

Billy the Kid and members of his gang from New Mexico also rode into the area from Canyon Diablo looking for a new place to hide, gamble, drink and carry on with women.

For a time, outlaws had virtual control of the whole area. A.F. Barnes, who for unknown reasons used an assumed name, said in the Territorial Legislature:

> "I am no angel and have seen most of the tough towns in the west, but Springerville was the worst of them all."

In the Newspaper from St Johns, Arizona on April 14, 1886 was the following item: Springerville, Arizona;

> "Ike Clanton shot a Mexican and in another incident, an unknown person burned Johnson's Hotel and Saloon, also noted in the article was that Pete Slaughter discharged all of his bad men at once as soon as he arrived home from a trip to Texas, and that there has been in that town such an unusual reign of peace in that town that the people are growing fidgety and unsettled."

The Tenth Arizona Territorial Legislature created Apache County in 1879. At that time, it extended as far south as the Gila River and encompassed 20,940 rugged square miles. Law enforcement was in the hands of incompetent deputies and self-appointed vigilante gangs. The county government was in debt, corrupt and inefficient. Oddly enough, the first indictments served in the new county were not against murderers or thieves, but against the Graham and Tewksbury families, who were rival cattle and sheep families whose blood feud continued until the last man was killed in 1892 and was known as the Pleasant Valley War or the Graham vs Tewksbury feud.

Law-abiding citizens, particularly the Mormon settlers, who had been prevented from holding public office by some of the corrupt county officials, because of their belief of polygamy, rose up in protest and demanded the election of a man who inadvertently played a role which immortalized him in Western history, Commodore Perry Owens. Below is another newspaper article from St. Johns read as follows:

> "In 1886 the lawless element run riot in Apache County, precipitating a reign of terror. Mr. Owens was a last resort and was elected sheriff."

After Owens' election, his office being in the county capital of Holbrook, it and neighboring Springerville were cleaned up from the outlaw element who had reigned for over ten years. The outlaws disappeared almost overnight, having respect for Owens' famed ability with a six-shooter. The events surrounding his shootout with the Andy Cooper *(Cooper Blevins)* a known murderer, horse thief and cattle rustler was carried by all of the national newspapers and brought fame to him and to Arizona.

Below is a photo of the famous lawman Commodore Perry Owens that was found in our National Archives.

While Eagar had always been a Mormon town, Springerville, was predominantly Spanish-American and Catholic. Side by side, the two communities lived together with mutual respect and cooperation. Many of the descendents of the early Spanish-American settlers live in Springerville today, among them the Carillos, Bacas and the Silvas who migrated from Socorro, New Mexico.

Other families came and stayed; the Rudd's, Colter's, Murray's, Saffell's, Burche's and the Springer families. The first postmaster was C.F. Barnes, who took office in 1879. Three generations of the Becker family live and carry on business in Springerville. Gustav and Julius Becker came to America from Hanover, Germany. After working on a farm in Illinois, the adventurous boys went to Kansas City where they caught a sage bound for Santa Fe. From the Spanish-Americans they heard of the *"Sierra Blanca,"* the high country on which sheep and cattle grew fat in the summer. The Becker family upon arriving in Arizona opened a small commissary on the river for the few families of Spanish-American farmers that had settled in the area.

Every year the irascible Little Colorado River washed away the small farms. In 1878, twenty families from Arkansas came in ox-drawn wagons to settle in the area and to farm. The Becker brothers eventually set up a mercantile store in Springerville. The farmers raised their own vegetables and wheat for flour, but they sold their excess oats and barley. Three to five thousand pounds of grain usually were contracted to the U.S. Army stationed at Fort Apache.

The Becker brothers would send the government check to the First National Bank of Albuquerque, some three hundred miles away. The cash came back from Albuquerque to Holbrook, then by two-wheel oxen cart to Springerville. The shipments of money were staggered over many weeks, the wagons only carrying $500 a trip, because of the number of robbers living and working their trade in the area.

The earliest big cattle ranchers in the country were two Englishmen, Smith and Tea, along with James Stinson, who would later move his herd to Pleasant Valley and subsequently become a main figure that started the Pleasant Valley War.

In about 1880 the Becker brothers went into the cattle business with Sherlock using the E L C brand. Gustav Becker had nine children who were sent away to be educated. Besides the mercantile and cattle business, they have been Ford dealers for fifty years, Standard Oil dealers and wholesale distributors.

Round Valley is thriving these days, it is the gateway to the White Mountain recreation area, bustling with tourists in the summer and a year round meeting place for cattle and sheep ranchers. It has good motels, restaurants and service stations, a high school, district elementary schools, municipal hospital, federal building and churches of five denominations.

Thirty miles north of Springerville on the Little Colorado and Route 66, is the quiet, agricultural town of St. Johns, also rich in history. The first white man in the area had been John Walker, who carried express to troops at Fort Apache and had a cabin up the river. But the town really took off with the coming of Solomon Barth, who had emigrated from Poland at age thirteen and began his American business career with a pack on his back from which he sold dry goods.

After pushing a cart on foot from the East to Utah with a band of Mormons, establishing a mercantile business in San Francisco, fighting with the Confederate guerillas known as Quantrellas' in Tucson, hauling gold ore from Yarnell, contracting mail with the Pony Express, trading with the Apaches and once being robbed, stripped and left to walk over a hundred miles by a band of Chiricahua Apaches under the leadership of their chief Cochise, Solomon Barth at last settled down to being a freighter, moving grain between Dodge City, Kansas and Fort Apache. He and his brothers, Morris and Nathan, had thirty-eight Murphy wagons with four yoke of oxen each. The wagon train hauled grain and hay all the way from Kansas through Albuquerque,

El Morro, Zuni, and crossed the Little Colorado at St. Johns before going into the White Mountains. The government paid ten cents a pound for oats, barley and corn and fifty dollars a ton for hay.

Below is a photo of a Murphy Freight Wagon and a Stagecoach to give the reader an idea of the size of a freight wagon. This photo was found in our National Archives.

Solomon Barth first saw the Little Colorado River Valley in 1867 when he acted as a guide for the survey party of the Atlantic & Pacific Railroad. The route followed the Little Colorado instead of a more direct line because of the necessity of a constant water supply for the steam engines. Barth was convinced it would be more profitable to raise grain in the good soil along the river and cut the abundant natural grasses, so he left at his home in Cubero, New Mexico in 1871 he came back to the Little Colorado Valley. He traveled with group of Mexican families, most of who had been his ox-drovers, and settled at a rocky crossing on the Little Colorado known as El Puente.

By 1875 another colony had been established by more settlers from the Rio Grande Valley under the leadership of Don Antonio Gonzales and Don Jose Garcia, but the Barth colony retained squatters' rights to the land and the water. The settlement was called El Vadito, the little crossing.

In 1874 Sol Barth married Refugia Landazo of Cubero and built an adobe home for her which later became the famous old Barth Hotel, still standing on the main street of St. Johns, filled with antique furniture, china, paintings, old photographs and an exceptional collection of Indian baskets, pottery and artifacts. El Vadito was re-named San Juan in honor of Senora Maria San Juan Baca de Padilla, the first white woman to live there, and was dedicated to San Juan Bautista. However, the postmaster general took a dim view of the un-American name and anglicized it to St. Johns in 1880.

Upstream from St. Johns, about seventeen miles north of Springerville, off Route 66 is the open grazing country studded with black malapai rock, is Lyman Lake, which was a reclamation project of 15,000 acres stocked with trout. The history of Lyman Lake reservoir goes back to 1877 when Joseph Smith called Ammon Tenney of Kanab to accompany Mormon scout Jacob Hamblin on an expedition to locate sites along the Little Colorado suitable for colonization. During the arduous journey, those farsighted men chose the towns of St. Johns, Concho, the Meadows and Woodruff.

Under the leadership of David K. Udall, the Mormons bought their land from Sol Barth for 770 cows and $2,000 in goods. The first payment was made with their tithing stock. After some deliberation, the water rights were settled at 3/5 for the Mormons and 2/5 for the Mexican people. By March 1880, 190 Mormons lived in the St. Johns Ward. A log schoolhouse was built in 1881 and Anna Romney was the first schoolteacher. Many of the men found work with the railroad then being built across the Northern Arizona Territory. Soon the Udall's built a cooperative mercantile store; a flour mill and a cattle herd all were leaked through the beds of quicksand established.

Still the river was unbridled, flooding its banks in spring and dwindling to a small trickle in early summer. By 1905 a dam at Salado Springs south of St. John was completed. The heavy run-off caused by a record snow in the

White Mountains that melted rather quickly due to a warm spring climate caused a leak through the beds of quicksand at the bottom of the dam and the structure washed out. With renewed faith, the Mormons once again began construction of a dam that was necessary to irrigate their lands. This time they chose an area twelve miles upstream at which point the river was running through a narrow area that was surrounded by a sold rock ridge on both sides of the river. The river ran over bedrock so the new dam had a better foundation and would not be washed out by future snow runoff or heavy rains.

The year 1915 was an exceptionally rainy year. Gradually the Little Colorado River swelled again and filled the lake to the brim. It finally overflowed its banks. The pressure was so great that Lyman Dam broke again, drowning eight people in the deluge. The surrounding farms were washed out from the flood. Several miles downstream, the dam at Woodruff finally broke from the pressure of the flow of water that had been held behind the Lyman Dam. Summer fields dried up and crops shriveled. Water from a nearby spring sold for high price of five cents a bucket. In 1923 a new dam was completed in the same area.

Below is a photo of Lyman Lake, found on the Hiking.com website. The dam is located at the end of the ridge.

Fifteen miles west of St. Johns on Interstate 180 lay the old Mexican town of Concho, cradled in the hills, now almost deserted except for a few small farms with bright chilies hanging from the adobe walls, a cantina with geraniums in the window, a gas station, post office and library. Solomon Barth won about eight thousand head of sheep in a poker game in Las Lunas. He put them in a range near Concho under the management of sheepherder Manuel Candalria and his family. The sheep industry grew as did the Candalaria family, until Concho was a bustling, prosperous trading center, supported by three banks.

These days Concho is a sleepy but picturesque village of abandoned adobes. North of Concho, near the Mormon settlement of Hunt, the Zuni River empties into the Little Colorado River, carrying with its load of silt, along with the memories of the pride, bravery, horsemanship and flashing steel that accompanied the men of the early Conquistador expeditions.

In 1539, Fray Marcos de Niza, after an expedition into the unexplored North, reported to Spanish authorities in Mexico that the seven cities of Cibola were rich in gold, silver and turquoise. For years, the Spaniards had listened to Indian myths concerning the seven fabled cities. They had found untold wealth in Mexico and Peru so why not in the North as well?

In the year 1540 an exploring party of 300 soldiers, along with several hundred Indians, including a herd of excellent horses, a herd of sheep and a herd of cattle, left Mexico under the leadership of Francisco Vasquez de Coronado. Instead of riches, they found the pueblo of Zuni, its rock houses three stories high built on hills. The windows, from thin sheets of mica, shimmered like pure gold in the New Mexico sun.

In 1692 Don Diego Vargas re-conquered the Zuni Indians living in the area without bloodshed, because they had been weakened by European diseases, disruption of their government and attacks by Navajos, Apaches and Utes, who by that time had learned to use the Spaniard's greatest weapon of conquest, the horse. It must be explained though that the Zuni were mostly farmers and makers of blankets and pottery. They were not a warlike people. So they were an easy target for raiding parties of their enemies. In fact, the Zuni are the oldest tribe in eastern Arizona and Western New Mexico. When the Anasazi, Hohokam and Mogollon Native Americans left the Southwest in 1350 because of a hundred year drought, the Zuni stayed, dug wells and survived, making them the oldest tribe still living here. They irrigated their land and grew crops from their well water. They still are a completely independent tribe. In fact the Santa Fe style homes made of Adobe and logs originated from the Zuni culture, as seen in the photo on the previous page.

Below is a photo of an Zuni village, circa 1900, that the author found in our National Archives

Between 1821 and 1848 Mexican rule replaced Spanish. When the United States won the territory from Mexico a fort was established nearby at Wingate. From Wingate, Lieutenant Beale's famed and highly unsuccessful Camel Corps passed through the Zuni area in 1857, leaving unhappy descendents to roam aimlessly along the Zuni and the Little Colorado River for years afterward.

Strengthened by the Carrizo and Zuni washes, the Little Colorado winds westward through cattle country south of the Petrified Forest. Milo Willbank wrote;

> *"It has been said that God placed the Petrified Forest beside the Little Colorado because it is the only river in the world muddy enough to float a petrified log."*

Chapter Two

160 million years ago, Northeastern Arizona was a low-lying basin with shifting streams that carried great logs from surrounding highlands along with gravel, sand and volcanic ash. During this period, huge trees, similar to pines now found in Australia and South America grew along our swamps, rivers and sea's. Eventually the logs were buried under silt deposits on the bottom of shallow seas.

This silt, under pressure, became layers of rock hundreds of feet thick. Mineral laden water filtered into the logs replacing the wood with mineral and turning them to stone. Over the past sixty million years, the area has risen thousands of feet and running water has eroded layer after layer of rock, finally exposing the petrified wood.

The general uplift of the Colorado Plateau to a height of six to eight thousand feet above sea level causing the cutting of the mighty Grand Canyon started about seven million years ago. This was in all probability the origin of the Little Colorado River. Extensive volcanic activity of the Pleistocene era during the last million years altered the old drainage patterns.

Below Holbrook the Little Colorado River is dammed once more, held gently by an old rock dam at the Mormon town of Woodruff. It is a peaceful place with water running lazily over the spillway while cows stand on the grassy banks of the reservoir drinking the reddish water.

Nathan Tenney and his family were the first settlers who arrived in the area in 1875. Not long after other pioneers arrived, built canals, houses and dams which were washed out time and time again. In 1879 the town was named Woodruff in honor of the president of the Mormon Church. The land was purchased from the railroad for eight dollars an acre in 1882 and the town laid out in four acre blocks with wide streets between.

North of the town lay the green, yellow and brown checkerboards of farm land extending to Blue Butte, a volcanic cone sacred to the Navajo who came there to cut jimsonweed for their ceremonies. Today Woodruff is still a small, serene oasis in the desert. Her men commute to jobs in nearby towns, but return at night to the sanctuary of their old-fashioned red brick houses amidst towering elms and cottonwoods.

Silver Creek, a tributary beginning in the White Mountains, flows gently down through the junipers and pinions of the Bourbon Ranch, past the valley of Shumway and through the Mormon towns of Snowflake and Taylor, to irrigate farms and gardens.

From Woodruff the Little Colorado River continues northward until it meets the erratic, side winding Puerco River. At the confluence of these two rivers lies a town once known as Horsehead Crossing. It is here, where the river is ugly, muddy and treacherous. A narrow bridge crosses the river, traffic is sometimes held up for hours by bands of sheep which must cross the river to reach the railroad, or pastures north of town. Basque and Spanish herders yell, toss rocks and wave their arms. Australian shepherd dogs yap at the heels of the sheep until, at last, some brave goat leads the way and the band follows.

Down along the river bank the Navajo men gather to gossip and sleep off their hangovers and start new ones. In the summer, when the river is full, laborers fish for catfish off the sides of the bridge. In the days before trucking, ranchers drove their cattle across the river to the railhead, riding hard and fast to keep them from bogging down in the patches of quicksand.

Holbrook consisted of a small trading post down on the crossing, run by Berardo and Padilla until the Atlantic and Pacific Railroad arrived to change the face of the whole country. In 1881 the first train arrived on its way from San Bernardino to Albuquerque, turning Holbrook into a hell-raising cattle town.

West of Holbrook the Leroux and Cottonwood creeks join the Little Colorado from the north, and Chevelon, Clear Creek, and Jack's Canyon flow in from the Mogollon Rim in the south. Along every creek, wash, and tributary, are the traces of a people who once inhabited Northeastern Arizona. They were the Aasazi, a Navajo word meaning *"the ancient ones."* Prior to the last Ice Age, man had already begun the series of migrations across the Bering Straits which led him through Canada, the Pacific Northwest and into the high, dry plateau of Northern Arizona. Between 400 and 500 A.D., people of the Modified Basket maker period moved into the Little Colorado drainage basin.

They lived in villages in homes called pit houses. The earliest structures were circular; the shape being retained to this day as ceremonial chambers called kivas used by the Hopi. During the later Pueblo Period, large communities developed a complex culture and thrived. From 700 to 1300 A.D. cliff dwelling were built along canyon walls as well as villages with unit houses along the banks of almost every river and stream. Pottery developed into a fine art, cotton was introduced, cloth woven, domestic turkeys were introduced, squash, corn and beans cultivated. By 1300 the whole northern plateau had been abandoned for reasons historians have never been able to discover.

Between 1276 and 1299 the Southwest and suffered a prolonged drought. The water table lowered and the streams dried up. The pueblo people including the Hohokam, Anasazi Mogollon and the Sinagua, for the most part farmers abandoned the Southwest, probably due to the drought. The Zuni, who lived and still live today, located in Eastern Arizona and Western New Mexico, mostly on the south side of Interstate 40, stayed during this drought. They are considered Pueblo people because they live in communities, as mentioned in the previous chapter.

The Spaniards began arriving in 1540, once more scattering the Native Arizona people. All along the Little Colorado, at intervals, are the rock symbols called petroglyphs, tumbled rocks and pottery fragments, which remind us of thousands of human beings whose cultures are gone forever.

Ten miles downstream from Holbrook is Joseph City, one of four sites chosen by Mormon explorers in the area. This, the oldest town in Navajo County, was first called Allen's Camp, Adele Westover and J. Morris Richard's book *"Unflinching Courage"* states;

> *"The Indians were not their worst enemy, they found, but Northeastern Arizona's arid climate, the sandstorms, the floods that came in rainy seasons to wash out their crude dams on the Little Colorado River, and the vast distances from all sources of supply of the necessities of life."*

Before the present dam was built, the rampaging Little Colorado River had washed out fourteen other families. But the people endured and stayed, as did the other Mormon settlers along the river, who raised livestock, built dairies, were farmers and some ran small local businesses.

The river crosses Route 66 near Winslow, a prosperous railroad town with a current population of about 10,000. In 1851 Captain Lorenzo Sitgreaves, led a twenty-man party of civil engineers down the Little Colorado River basin under contract with the army to establish a route for the military to use to transport freight. Winslow at that time had no permanent settlers living there until the coming of the Atlantic & Pacific Railroad in 1881. There was really no real growth to speak of until it became a main terminal and roundhouse and engine switching and storage area for the Santa Fe Railroad that purchased the Atlantic & Pacific Railroad. The town was named after General Edward Winslow who was the president of the Atlantic and Pacific Railroad.

Winslow in those days was a dusty ramshackle town with several small privately owned businesses, a hundred or so frame cottages, and a Chinese restaurant and as always in railroad or mining towns, several saloons, and gambling houses and last but not least several brothels, of which all were located along Front Street on both sides of the railroad tracks.

There was a woman who grew up in Winslow at that time that was interviewed by a local newspaper and who went on record as saying;

> *"My mother grew up in the east and we were raised Baptists. She told us to hurry home from school each day and as we passed the saloons and the brothels in the red light district, to keep our heads down and not look up to draw attention to*

ourselves. Of course as we passed the red light district every day on our way home we looked up the whole way past the saloons and brothels. We were so engrossed in looking at all the action from the saloons and brothels that sometimes we would trip and fall because we were not watching where we were going."

"Doc" Demerest was the first white settler in Winslow and he opened a hotel. J.H. Breed arrived a few months after Demerest and he built a rock trading post. Then Mrs. Mary Downs came to Winslow. She was a widow from Santa Fe who opened Downs House. She was a midwife and also doubled as the community's undertaker. By the turn of the century, Winslow was a sprawling, booming, roughhouse railhead and cattle shipping center.

With the opening of the Harvey House, passengers on the Santa Fe could stop, stretch and have dinner on white linens, fine china dinnerware and fine silver utensils. The Harvey House hired hearty and virtuous, single girls from the East and Midwest, who were looking for adventure, a husband or simply to escape the drudgery of farm chores or the boredom of living in the small eastern towns to work as waitresses at the Harvey House. Their wages were $1.00 per day, plus room, board and laundry. Their wages were about the same pay scale as a cowboy working the range. They were required to be in at 9 pm each night, and their behavior was zealously watched. Local business owners' wives and church ladies complained bitterly to the railroad if any

Below is a photo of a typical Harvey House. This one was located in Winslow, Arizona. This photo was found in our National Archives and is public domain.

From Winslow, thousands of cattle and sheep were shipped east to Kansas City and Omaha. In those days the owners had to accompany the stock to the eastern markets so they could negotiate the sale of their stock. They would sleep at night in the caboose. Then during the day they would walk along the top of the Palace Stock Cars, frequently going down into the *"manholes"* to help any cattle that had fallen before they were trampled. Every thirty-six hours the stock was let out to obtain water and hay. Then the stock driven back into the railroad cars with prod poles supplied by the railroad.

To the North from Winslow, the Little Colorado River broadens. In dry seasons is a thread of red winding water along the cracked river bed. After the last summer rains, the rivers roar across the open country, foaming white above the dark water. North it continuers to flow toward the Navajo reservation into Navajo country, traveling through a long a deep canyon on its way north passing what remains of ghost towns, Two Guns, Canyon Diablo and Wolf Post. Just past Wolf crossing the river widens going through the empty red earth and dark blue mesas along the Navajo Reservation. Here and their along its banks, Navajo squaws and children herd sheep, hogs and cattle to the river, while braves water their horses. A woman in a velvet blue blouse with a brown satin skirt hauls water from the river to her Hogan in a horse drawn wagon.

Extending for over three hundred miles along the north bank of the Little Colorado is a vast stretch of delicately colored buttes, mesas and canyons which change from the gold of morning to rose to reddish brown, magenta and deep violent as the sun's rays slant and the shadows shift. This subtly sculptured landscape, part of the Chinle formation, is one of America's best known physical features of the Painted Desert.

Near the Navajo village of Leupp, dozens of washes from the northeastern reaches of the Navajo Reservation converge and flow into the Little Colorado as Oraibi Wash. From far beyond the three Hopi mesas they come. Out of the dim and fading past they bring the sacred water upon which the Hopi have based their religion and their lives for so many centuries. The village of Orabi itself is the oldest continuously inhabited town in the United States. Strange sounding names on the map such as Mishongnovi, Shipaulovi, and Shimopavi, designate the Hopi villages built of native sandstone high atop the three great fingers of Black Mesa.

For about 800 years the Hopi have maintained their ancient and complex culture in spite of the effects of drought, disease, starvation, attacks by their enemies, along with misunderstandings from Government agents and attempts at conversion by Spanish priests, missionaries. Except for a rebellion against Spanish priests in 1680, they have lived peacefully with their Navajo neighbors. In their homeland, the Hopi practice alluvial farming of their traditional foods; corn, melons, beans, squash, sunflower seeds. Every year they hold ancient and meaningful ceremonies as supplications for rain and subsequent good crops.

Here in these vast and endless stretches of blue sky and red earth, the Little Colorado takes on some of the serenity, Stoicism and timelessness of Indian culture. *"To walk in beauty,"* is the Navajo life way. *"Hopi"* means *"peace."* So many people, so many centuries, have mingled here, along the lonely river in the lonely land.

In *"Sun Chief,"* the autobiography of a Hopi, Don Talayesva tells of those early frustrations when the government agents tried to make white men out of the Indians. But even in the bitterness and confusion of those turn-of-century days, were rare and touching moments of understanding between men. He tells of a Mormon crossing the Indian Reservation who hired four Hopi boys to dig a grave for his son;

> *"The Mormon and his wife came to the cemetery in a wagon loaded with a coffin, which was covered with expensive velvet. They cried and cried because this seventeen-year old boy was their only child and had come with them from Salt Lake City. Some of the government employees*

sang 'Nearer My God to Thee and Shall We Gather at the River?' The young Hopi boys felt sorry for the parents and joined in the singing. They filled the grave with earth and put stones at the head and feet. They thought to themselves that they did want to be buried in a coffin; even a fancy one covered in velvet, because it was sealed tightly and they thought there would be no way for their spirit to escape and join their ancestors."

Below is a photo of the Grand Falls on the Little Colorado River, located near a trading post was found in our National Archives.

Northwest of Leupp, the river, when full, provides one of the most spectacular sights in Arizona. Thirty- miles northeast of Flagstaff are the Grand Falls, a series of sandstone steps about three hundred feet across, which create a foaming waterfall. The stream flow of the Little Colorado at Grand Falls has been recorded since 1914 to determine the river's hydrological importance. The maximum recorded flow during that time was 586,000 acre feet in 1941 and the lowest was 71,000 acre feet in 1934.

Of greater concern is the heavy load of silt this narrow, the swift moving and ungovernable stream carries with here. The estimated average annual silt flow is 27,500 acre feet. Quoting P.E. Coe, head area engineer for the B&R. The U.S. Bureau of Reclamation was in charge of construction of a dam on the Little Colorado River at the Coconino site, approximately eight miles northwest of Cameron, Arizona. The purpose of the structure would be flood control, silt control, recreation and fish and wildlife conservation. No power facilities would be installed. The silt control function would be particularly important since the reservoir would retain sediment which would otherwise be deposited behind Bridge Canyon Dam.

One of the founding families in the area whose history parallels the history of Yavapai County was the Babbitts'. David and William Babbitt sold their small grocery store in Cincinnati, Ohio in hopes of following their dream of going west. They got off the train in Santa Fe train in Flagstaff, Arizona in 1886 but saw a discouraging row of frame shacks along a mud rutted road. Timber, cattle, sheep, railroading and saloons were the town's main industries. Before long, the Babbitt brothers acquired a Navajo trading post as well as their small store. A man named Dittenhoffer, who owned the trading post at Red Lake near Oraibi Wash, was shot and killed in a fight over a game of cards. The Babbitts, whom he owed money to for goods they bought on credit, acquired the post as payment of his debt to them. Their mercantile store was prospering by 1889, Ads in the Coconino Sun newspaper read as follows;

> "Dave Babbitt, a dealer in hardware, stoves, paints, oils, cement, plaster of Paris, guns and ammunition, says that business is booming."

In 1889 they bought the remnant of the A-1 Bar brand and cattle that went with the brand owned by the Arizona Cattle Company and run by a man with the singular name of Captain Bullwinkle. The combination mercantile and cattle business kept the firm going through several depressions. The businesses are still in the family and they own and manage businesses in Winslow, Holbrook, Williams, Kingman, Page, Prescott and the Grand Canyon. They also manage cattle ranches in Arizona and Montana.

North of Flagstaff the river skirts the edge of Wupatki National Monument, which is a series of prehistoric apartment house villages of the Great Pueblo Period. Wupatki is not far from the Sunset Crater, a volcanic cone which has erupted within the tenure of man. The Little Colorado flows under the suspension bridge at Cameron on Interstate 89, rushing toward one final spree before she reaches her rendezvous with the big Colorado River. About fifteen miles off Interstate 89, on the Grand Canyon road, Is a good viewpoint of the Little Colorado River gorge. She has begun the same violent erosion and cutting which formed the mighty Grand Canyon.

>**Below is a photo of the Cameron Trading Post at the turn of the 20th century. This photo was found in our National Archives.**

At a point about seven miles below Cameron, this wild and undisciplined river begins its last tortuous forty one miles to where it meets the Big Colorado River.

Although a handful of prospectors, Indians, scientists, and photographers have seen the gorge, perhaps only one man in the world has first hand knowledge of this inaccessible and formidable canyon. Dr. J. H. Butchart, a retired mathematics professor at Arizona State University, who made several expeditions into the gorge and walked nearly all of the bed from the mouth of river to Cameron.

Two main trails lead into the Little Colorado gorge, the Blue Spring Trail and the Salt Trail, which is closer to the mouth. From the barren, rocky and winding plateau the trail begins a descent of 3400 feet to the bottom. From the Kaibab limestone of the plateau, the scarcely perceptible trail, marked at intervals with rock cairns, winds down the loose talus past the Coconino sandstone, Hermit Shale, the 800-foot thick red Supai, the 550-foot thick Red Wall dyed by iron oxides from above, down past the Cambrian Tonto formation, the Tapeats sandstone, finally to reach the Algonkian at the bottom, the earliest form of sedimentary rock.

Until 1912 the Hopi made an annual pilgrimage, using this trail, to sacred salt deposits near the mouth. The fascinating details of this Hopi Salt Expedition are described in the book "Sun Chief," in which the author says;

> "The salt lies in dangerous territory, and long ago the War Twins had set up shrines and established rules to make the journey safe for the Hopi."

With their pathos, prayer feathers, the group made its way from Moenkopi to this eerie and forbidding area, the mythological home of departed spirits. At an ancient shrine of rock inscriptions, he wrote;

> "I prayed earnestly, realizing that we were entering the land of spirits and would have to cope with strange powers."

I thought about the time I looked down that same trail and unconsciously crossed myself before starting out. Atop an abyss which seems like the edge of the world, he said;

> "I looked into the canyon, which seemed miles deep, and saw the Little Colorado shinning from the bottom. I was frightened and I wondered if we would ever return in safety."

Upstream from the bottom of the Salt Trail are cataracts and blue travertine springs.

While the water is safe to drink, it has a disagreeable taste, according to the writer Gladwell Richardson in one of his articles;

> *"The water tastes like a mixture of table salt and Epsom salts."*

The photo below of the Little Colorado at the Salt Trail in Canyon Diablo was taken by the author's friend Jeff Dunn

At the base of the canyon wall is a shallow cave which was a shrine of the Hopi god of fire and death, Masau'u. Not far downstream is the most sacred place of all, chocolate-colored cone twenty-five-yards wide at which bubbles yellow, gaseous water. This is the original sipapu of Hopi legend, the place where all of mankind once emerged from the underworld.

Further downstream, along a rugged trail probably made by Bighorn sheep, is a stone building under an over-hanging cliff, all that remains of a prospector's house known as Beamer's Cabin. At the confluence of the two rivers, Cape Solitude towers 3400 feet above the chasm. And here the waters of the Little Colorado, fed by travertine springs, are a deep, pure turquoise, most sacred color of the Indians, as they join the muddy brown Colorado.

Chapter Three

When John Clum, the Indian Agent at the San Carlos Apache Reservation, left in the winter of 1877 it was prosperous. From when he arrived in 1874 to when he left he formed a tribal council of chiefs that basically ran the reservation. Their own Apache police were in charge of running the agency and doing a great job. He had ten to fifteen Apache Scouts that had enlisted in the Army and helped him track down Apaches that jumped the reservation and bring them back. He designed and had the Indians build a series of dams along the Gila River. Then he had them build canals to carry the lake water to their fields to irrigate their crops and livestock. Crops and livestock flourished while he was the Indian Agent.

The previous agents and agents that came to San Carlos after Clum left shorted the Indians on their rations and livestock. They sold the items to traders to profit themselves at the expense of the Indians. At first the tribal leaders had their doubts about Clum. They called him Nantan (leader in the Apache language) be-tunny-kah-yen (Man with a high forehead) because Clum was going bald at an early age. In fact, being partially bald was a good thing to the Apaches. They felt he was a man of great intelligence. After getting to know him they council of chiefs came to love and respect him. He told them right off in their first meeting that it was his plan that they run their own reservation and it was also his goal to have the army move off the reservation entirely.

John Clum pictured with several reservation Apaches soon after his arrival at the San Carlos Reservation. This photo was found in our National Archives.

John Clum took a job in Tucson with the Daily Star newspaper and worked there as a reporter for about a year then he moved to Tombstone where he started the Tombstone Epitapth newspaper, which is still in existence today. He eventually became mayor of Tombstone and was a lifelong friend of Wyatt Earp and his brothers.

It was just a little before Clum departed San Carlos that they reservation started to endure a two-year drought. Eventually the lakes dried up causing all of their crops to die. Disease and pestilence abounded the whole reservation. Tempers flared and Apaches were dying on a daily basis. Under such terrible conditions it was no surprise that the Apaches started to escape from the reservation.

Another photo found in the National Archives taken while the building of one of the canals in the mid 1870's at the San Carlos Apache Reservation

It was in the summer of 1878 when Naiche, also known as crooked jaw, because his jaw bones were not symmetrical. Naiche was the son of Cochise and served as the current chief of the Chiriachaua Apache Nation. He took Fifty-five bronco Apache braves, consisting of Chirichaua, Warm Springs and White Mountain Apaches and jumped the reservation. Ticked off at everybody, they went on the warpath. They headed north along Cherry Creek past the small town of Young, Arizona and then just below the Mogollon Rim they headed west along the East Verde River with their ultimate goal to follow the Mogollon Rim trails to the Navajo Reservation so they could raid their villages stealing valuable Navajo blankets and pottery.

Along the way they raided ranches, farms and small villages killing everyone they came across and stealing booty from their victims. This actually was the way of life the Chirichaua Apaches lived for hundreds of years. Most Apache nations were actually farmers and ranchers except for the Chirichaua tribe that originated in southeastern Arizona between Tombstone and the New Mexico/Arizona border and the Warm Springs Apaches who lived in Southwestern New Mexico. For whatever reason they two tribes got along. They stole cattle and horses from ranchers here in the USA and then took them south through Skeleton Canyon into Old Mexico where they sold their herds to the Mexican Army or Mexican Traders. Then they would steal

Cattle and Horses from the Mexicans and herd them back through Skeleton Canyon to the USA and sell the stock to the US Army or Traders.

Their ultimate goal of the raiding Apaches was to find a hiding place somewhere near the Navajo Reservation that started just north of the Little Colorado River, from where they could raid the nearby unsuspecting villages, killing the inhabitants of whole villages, taking slaves, stealing livestock, harvested crops and other items they could trade with the Mexicans.

Their plan was to jump into the Little Colorado River basin and follow it through Canyon Diablo to somewhere near Wolf Crossing. The Navajo Reservation started on the other side of Wolf Crossing on the Little Colorado. As they rode up Canyon Diablo, somewhere near the town of Two Guns, which was up on top of the mesa, they discovered a perfect hiding place.

As they rode toward Wolf Crossing in a north westerly direction in the canyon they noticed the entrance to a cave. The entrance was at the bottom of the canyon and it was only visible riding north east and it could not be seen if riding from the opposite direction unless a person just happened to look back. It was also not visible from the top of the mesa on each side of the canyon.

A closer look by scouts and upon reporting back to Naiche, they told him that the cave was large enough for them to hide themselves, their ponies and stolen booty. There were several large rooms that they could use as corrals. The scouts also reported that there were several fissures that came all the way from the top of the mesa that provided the cave with constant fresh air. They would be able to light fires to keep them warm in the winter months. They cave was at a constant 68- degree temperature through the summer and winter months. They told Naiche that after exploring the cave that it was over three miles long but the larger rooms were within a few yards from the entrance. The cave provided the Apaches a perfect hiding place from where they could move in raiding parties to several Navajo villages that were within thirty miles of their hiding place and since it was not on the Navajo reservation the Navajo people did not even know it existed.

Naiche was born in 1857. As a young man, Naiche *(means "the Mischief Maker" or "Meddlesome One")* led many raids against white settlers. When his older brother Taza died of pneumonia in 1876 he became chief of the Chiricahua Apaches. In 1879, Naiche resisted relocation to the San Carlos Apache Reservation and went to Mexico with Geronimo's Band. While ensconced in the Sierra Madre south of Rio Grande, Naiche and Geronimo attacked American and Mexican communities with relative impunity. While Naiche was certainly the hereditary chief of the Chiricahua Apaches at this time, it appears that Geronimo was viewed as the great leader and probably persuaded Naiche, the younger man, to submit to his leadership during these campaigns. During the early 1880s, the U.S. Army relentlessly tracked the rebellious Chiricahua Apaches until Naiche surrendered on May 25, 1883, to General George Crook. For a while, Naiche and Geronimo languished at the San Carlos Reservation, but in 1885, the two leaders left with over one hundred men in a last attempt to avoid American control.

By the middle of September 1886, Apache scouts and detachments of the U.S. Army were able to force their surrender in the inhospitable terrain of Mexico. Soon after the Chiricahuas were captured, Naiche and Geronimo and their men were incarcerated first at Fort Marion, Florida, and then at Mount Vernon Barracks in Alberta. Although Naiche and his men wanted return home to Arizona, angry white settlers there prevented it. After

Kiowa and Comanche leaders invited the Chiricahua Apaches to share their reservation, Naiche and 295 other Apaches relocated to Fort Sill, Oklahoma, on October 4, 1895. Naiche remained in Oklahoma until 1913. He eventually returned to the Southwest, where he lived in peace for eight years, dying of influenza at Mescalero, New Mexico, in 1921. The irony is that Naiche with the influence of several religious missionaries became a Christian a few years before he passed into the happy hunting grounds.

Below is a picture of Chirachaua Chief Naiche with one of his wives and then the other picture is of Naiche taken just before he passed away in 1921.

Chapter Four

The history of the most unusual town of Two Guns which sits above the Death Cave is very near the half-way mark between Flagstaff and Winslow on Interstate Highway 40 is very interesting. The exit is well marked and what remains of the ghost town is only a mile from the highway and can easily be seen from the highway.

The surrounding area of the Coconino plateau's rolling ranges, ringed by distant mountains have played an important role in western history since the coming of the Dawn Men, the first aboriginal inhabitants. Following them were the Basket Makers, and then Pueblo I and Pueblo II periods, as shown by their typical cliff dwelling ruins in Canyon Diablo and its tributaries.

Potsherds recovered at Two Guns have been dated by the carbon method, placing the greatest density of inhabitants there as between 1050 and 1600 A. D. The centuries 1050 to 1300 saw the greatest Indian population that the region has ever had. This was due to fertile farming land on the plateau created by disintegration of the volcanic fields of lava and ashes that once spewed out of the San Francisco Mountains skyline west.

The chronicle of a Spanish party in 1769 is more definite. Recently this date was found by Melvin McCormick, cut with an inscription and a Christian cross into a huge rock on the Little Colorado River.

This party, composed of several padres and Spanish soldiers was an ill-fated one. The Franciscans, mined and collected a huge store of silver bars somewhere in central Arizona, then set out to transport the treasure by mule train to their church headquarters in Santa Fe over the Santa Fe Trail. Sadly, without the churches knowledge two years earlier in 1767 the Spanish crown had laid claim to all gold and silver found in the New World, so when they arrived back at their mission in Santa Fe, the Spanish soldiers confiscated the Silver ore.

As was mentioned in chapter two, the first official U.S. exploration of the area began in 1851. Captain Lorenzo Sitgreaves, the leader of a team of U.S. topographical Engineers, on a government contract, led an exploration party west from Santa Fe. Their objective was to determine if the Little Colorado was navigable to the west coast.

Both sides of Canyon Diablo were explored seeking a shorter and more direct crossing for a route passing south of the San Francisco

Peaks. Apparently Sitgreaves did not venture much farther upstream than the present trading post Two Guns. In his official report he recommended use of the old natural north crossing *(Wolf Crossing)*.

> **Below is a photo of Wolf Crossing on the Little Colorado River about twenty miles upstream from the Cameron Trading Post. This photo was taken when the river was high, most likely in the spring. The photo was found in our National Archives.**

In 1853, Captain Amiel W. Whipple, on his historic thirty-fifth parallel railroad survey for then Secretary of War Jefferson Davis, in the cabinet of then President Franklin Pierce, reached the edge of the deep gorge and dubbed it Canyon Diablo *(Devil's Canyon)*. Whipple wrote in his journal;

> *"We were all surprised to find at our feet, in magnesium limestone, a chasm probably two hundred fifty feet in depth, the sides precipitous,*

and about three hundred yards across the top. A thread-like rill of water could be seen below, but descent was impossible. A railroad bridge could be built and the banks of the canyon as canyon and surrounding area would provide plenty of stone and a solid foundation for this purpose."

Spaniards were passing continuously from New Mexico through the area from around 1750. The first American traders were known to have arrived was in 1825. They were beaver trappers, who did their trapping along the Little Colorado River, which until the late 1880's contained a heavy growth of cottonwood trees and willows that extended out into the mud flats. After the American occupation of the southwest, the regular route from the east in a direct line to the San Francisco Peaks on the horizon let traders and other travelers right to the level rim of the chasm known as Canyon Diablo. From the Indians the travelers would learn that access to water and a crossing could be reached a few miles down-stream. True, it was a fairly steep, rough route, but it was certainly more possible than the one they had first encountered. Along these walls hundreds of names were carved into the rocks.

In 1854, only one year after Whipple had been through this country and made his survey, Felix Aubrey, a Santa Fe trader, laid out the first wagon route eastward across northern Arizona, traveling from San Jose, California with sixty men to Santa Fe, New Mexico. When he reached the west rim of Canyon Diablo, he was baffled until Indians told him he could detour downstream. He then proceeded north along the rim to the regular crossing. While at Canyon Diablo, he met a large number of Indians, who traded him $1500 in gold nuggets for some old clothing and blankets, but wouldn't disclose the source of the gold. After reaching Santa Fe, he was killed in August of 1854 in a personal encounter. His route was known after that as the California-Santa Fe Trail.

The next major survey of the 35th parallel was the famous Beale Camel Experiment in 1857. Secretary of War Jefferson Davis was officially largely responsible for this seemingly bizarre endeavor of using camels to pack supplies and equipment from Fort Defiance, Arizona to California's eastern frontier. Seventy-nine camels, imported from the Middle East through Texas seaports. The party was led by Arab, Greek and Turkish camel drivers and commanded by colorful Ned Beale, later to become well known as the one who carried the news of the California gold strike to President Milliard Fillmore.

Lieutenant Edward F. Beale, no relation to Ned Beale, led the Beale Camel team of U.S. Topographical engineers across the California-Santa Fe trail on an assignment to open a wagon road from Fort Defiance, Arizona to California's eastern frontier reached the edge of Canyon Diablo on September 8, 1857.

In his official report Lieutenant Beale admitted that his guide through the country warned him that he could not cross this chasm so far south of the Little Colorado River, but he had to find out for himself, going north to the old trail. Having been convinced by trying, Beale was forced downstream to the barranca. This old trail was officially designated the Beale Road across Arizona. However, frontiersmen long using it continued to refer to the route as the California-Santa Fe Trail.

In the spring of 1858 Lieutenant J.C. Ives set out with another survey party from Needles, California, over the Beale Road to Fort Defiance. He attempted to cross the canyon higher upstream because it would be a short cut saving many miles of travel. In this venture he also failed.

During the winter of 1858-1859, Lieutenant Edward F. Beale returned to work on the road he had laid out. For a while he camped out with his party on Government Prairie north of Flagstaff, before removing his command to the west side of Canyon Diablo. One of several tumble-down building still dotting the landscape and visible from Two Guns was probably where he camped.

The following year he made another trip along the road he had laid out. This time he brought the camels again to pack his equipment. The outbreak of the Civil War in 1864 ended what had been a successful experiment with camels able to carry 700 pounds each and survive on the desert vegetation.

When the Navajo tribal roundup of 1864 began, many families fled into the main canyon and all along the side defiles ahead of the U.S. Cavalry. The cavalry brought with them hundreds of Indian enemies of the Navajo who were authorized by the military commanders in the field to take all the Navajo livestock they could find, or turn them into the army for monetary reward at so much per head.

Objecting to the U.S Cavalry's taking of their food and livestock, over eight thousand

Navajo Indians were taken into custody and imprisoned at Fort Sumner, New Mexico for four years. The Navajos who fled the Melgosa Desert into Canyon Diablo remained in hiding until their enemies left the country.

After the outbreak of the Civil War all exploration of the California-Santa Fe trail and the area around it was halted for several years. Soon after the war ended Herman Wolf returned to the canyon and the Little Colorado River to trap beaver. His first cabin camp was called the Beaver House *(Chi Bogan)* by the Navajo. They so gave it this name because his beaver pelts were always found leaning against the walls of his abode to dry. Later on the name was applied to the trading post.

Wolf probably built his large stockade picket post prior to 1868. But he was definitely in the trading business on the river downstream from the mouth of Canyon Diablo that year. For several years his outpost was the sole center of attraction in the little known frontier of northern Arizona along the California-Santa Fe trail. But there soon followed others who entered the wonderful country to stay. Meanwhile he and the U.S. Army were both fighting renegade Indians.

Wolf probably built his large stockade picket post prior to 1868. But he was definitely in the trading business on the river downstream from the mouth of Canyon Diablo that year. For several years his outpost was the sole center of attraction in the little known frontier of northern Arizona along the California-Santa Fe trail. But there soon followed others who entered the wonderful country to stay. Meanwhile he and the U.S. Army were both fighting renegade Indians.

Below is what is left of Wolf Trading Post on the south side of the Little Colorado River. This photo was taken by the author's friend Jeff Dunn and used in this book with his permission.

One of the first cavalry battles with Indians on the Little Colorado River Basin in Canyon Diablo occurred on April 18, 1867, according to records in the National Archives. Companies B and I, of the 8th Cavalry, under command of Captain J.M. Williams, pursued a band of Apaches from the Verde Valley over the Mogollon Rim and down Canyon Diablo's east side. In an engagement somewhere near Two Guns, thirty of the renegade Indians were killed.

Apaches when pursued north of the Mogollon Rim always fled to the safety of deep canyons. They had a mania for following the well marked ancient Navajo Trail, seeking refuge in Canyon Diablo into which they could descend afoot if attacked. Most of the engagements between the cavalry and Apaches were minor clashes with a few exceptions.

The greater portion of the Navajo Tribe was released from the prison reservation at Fort Sumner and returned to their old homes in 1868. Many families came down the Little Colorado basin into the Melgosa Desert. Many families came down the Little Colorado basin into the Melgosa Desert. They seemed to think that the mere presence of a white man at Wolf Post afforded them protection. Soon they moved south of the river onto old hunting grounds along both sides of Canyon Diablo.

The Apaches, discovering the permanent trading post established by Wolf, threw raiding parties against it in 1868 and 1869. Wolf, and the Santa Fe New Mexicans working for him at the time, repelled them all but not without some casualties.

On September 26, 1869, the Apaches and the cavalry fought another battle near Two Guns. Troops from Camp Verde, not identified in the records, took out after Apaches raiding north into Navajo country. Well ahead of the troopers, the Indians were returning south along Canyon Diablo loaded with loot when they encountered the cavalry. Following a short flight, the Apaches attempted to make their escape west into the San Francisco Mountains, the highest peaks in Arizona. Overtaken before they could reach the old crossing, thirty-six were killed and twelve were captured. On soldier was reported as being wounded in the battle.

All through the 1870's more Apache raiders struck Wolf Post. By then the Navajos were increasing in numbers and rallied to help drive the enemy away from their friend Herman Wolf with whom they had become dependent on for trading their blankets, jewelry and other goods for tobacco, wheat, sugar and other items they needed to survive.

Mormon explores from Utah reconnoitered the Melgosa Desert through the valley of the Little Colorado in 1874, seeking irrigable land for settlement. This reconnaissance resulted in the first crossing of the Kaibab limestone gorge at Two Guns two years later. Bishop Lot Smith of the Mormon Church headed five colonies which settled in the lower Little Colorado basin.

From three of those settlements, Ballinger and Sunset near present day Winslow, and Joseph City, he laid out a road southwest to Mormon Lake a little south of Flagstaff. In 1876 he established a co-operative dairy herd, a cheese making plant and he also built a sawmill. This route, leaving the river at Winslow, passed in an almost direct line through Sunset Gap, south of the Meteor Crater, across the canyon above Two Guns and past Kinnikinick Lake to Mormon Lake. Over this road moved wagons, buckboards, herds of cattle, pack outfits and usual number of mounted travelers.

Before long Smith's road became a gateway for stockmen. They established the first ranches in northern Arizona and soon appeared in increasing numbers, occupying the range around Two Guns. The first such was 800 head trailed in by James M. Baker to Canyon Diablo headwaters. He stayed north of the military road that had been laid out along the Mogollon rim from Fort Apache west to Forts Verde and Whipple.

For some reason Baker, for whom Baker Butte was named, remained only three years before moving onto the Salt River Valley in central Arizona. The year of his arrival in Arizona, 1877, John Wood brought a small herd over from New Mexico. His cattle grazed south of Two Guns where herds of antelope run, and west into the Coconino National Forest. Wood shifted his grazing cattle depending on whether or not raiding Indians reported coming his way. The third cattleman to arrive with a herd was August Helzer from Utah. These men were the pioneer cattle ranchers of the many who followed the railroad through Arizona in 1881-1882, and overran the countryside along it.

Navajos had long used the Two Gun ranges for summer and fall grazing for their sheep, cattle and horses. In those days the present naked, red clay flats were covered with a thick grass sod, the bunch types and the grammas.

The first white owned sheep reaching the Two Guns country were migratory flocks from New Mexico in the late 1860's to about 1874. Moving slowly down the Little Colorado, they turned out of the basin, grazed until fall along Canyon Diablo and hen returned to New Mexico. Extended droughts in California in the early 1870's brought a number of sheep owners into the area. Their advance scouts hunting grass and water, discovered the region fulfilled their needs.

While a number of small flocks preceded him, John Clark drifted in with 3000 head of sheep in 1875. He was the first big sheep herder of importance to settle in Clark Valley, now known as Lake Mary, for winter rang and Two Guns for the summer and fall grazing. After Clark, came William Ashurst, the father of Senator Henry F. Ashurst, in 1876. Locating south at Ashurst Run, he used Canyon Diablo ranges part of the time.

That same year brothers J.F and W.A. Daggs trailed more than ten thousand sheep into northern Arizona from California. Their grazing camps were strung out from each headquarters past Two Guns north to the Little Colorado.

In the winter of 1874 a scouting troop of cavalry soldiers rode through Chavez Pass onto a horrible scene. Apaches had attacked and almost completely destroyed a wagon train of immigrants near the military road. The identity of no one in the train was ever discovered. Information found at the scene indicated they were on their way to Prescott.

Their stock had been run off, and the wagons with their contents set on fire. Only the metal used in their construction remained amid the debris of the fires. Bodies of murdered men, women and children had been thrown into the flames. All the fragments of charred bones raked out of the ashes were buried in a common grave. It was estimated that twenty-eight human beings were massacred.

Plans for a railroad to the west were put on hold until the 1880's, and the camels were sold or escaped into the wild. Some of the camels were seen in the area as late as 1900. Beale's Camel Road remained the basis for the 1920's National Old Trail Highway, which we know as Route 66, or, for the younger folks, U.S. Interstate 40.

The more recent history of local Indian tribes reveals that they used the canyon both as a refuge from enemies and as a vantage point from which to launch attacks.

The Apache and Navajo tribes often employed the area as a battleground, even after the arrival of white men in the southwest. From the earliest years of settling in what is now Arizona, the Navajos used a well-traveled trail from the north passing along the east side of Canyon Diablo past Two Guns. It went through Chavez Pass and over the stark Mogollon Rim into central Arizona.

Hearing from Hopi Indians of a great canyon and river far to the west, Coronado dispatched Cardenas to discover it. Led by Hopi guides, the small party came down from the mesa villages to the Little Colorado River. Undoubtedly they crossed at ancient Hopi Ford, somewhere between Winslow and Leupp.

The party turned northwest in order to pass above the San Francisco Peaks on the blue skyline. Following downstream, they crossed Canyon Diablo near where it enters the river on the flatland. The party was Captain Juan Melgosa arrived at the edge of Grand Canyon but failed in an attempt to descend into the mighty gorge to the Colorado River. The upper end of the Painted Desert, from Leupp to north of Cameron, was named after the Spanish explorer and called the Melgosa Desert.

Spanish explorers of 1542 may have provided the name for the fantastic defile at Two Guns, calling it Canon Diablo aka; the Devil's Canyon. If so, they certainly came part way upstream along the sharp rim to where sheer walls made a crossing impossible.

It is historically uncertain whether this party of Spaniards, or that of Antonio de Espejo, aptly named the canyon in 1582. That autumn Espejo set out from Zuni accompanied by nine men on a silver prospecting expedition.

Proceeding west to the Hopi villages they visited Walpi, Shungopovi, Mishongovi, Oraibi and Awatobi. From the latter pueblo not on a mesa, Espejo took four of his men and Hopi guides' southward, exploring new country.

After crossing the Little Colorado River, they came in against Canyon Diablo off the Navajo Trail somewhere near Two Guns. The vertical walls preventing a crossing, they continued on up the east side. Passing somewhere south of Kinnikinick Lake they reached Stoneman Lake, proceeding from there into the Verde Valley of central Arizona

The pueblos of New Mexico, including the Hopi of Arizona, rebelled and drove out their Spanish conquerors in 1680. Twelve years later Don Diego de Vargas came with another expedition north from Mexico. In New Mexico he finally conquered the rebellious Indians.

After accomplishing this task, he set forth hunting valuable metals, mercury, gold and silver the Indians told him about. Several of his small parties explored west and south from the Hopi villages. They did make a few but not important discoveries.

It was during this period that the extensive legend of the "*Lost Mines of the Padres*" originated. Men still seek these legendary and fabulous mines. From the translated ancient Spanish documents, they could be anywhere from Two Guns west to the Colorado River or north to Utah's Blue Mountains.

Their several reports of the mines resulted in many unauthorized expeditions of wealth seekers venturing west from New Mexico. Although not authenticated by any records and identity, most of them crossed Canyon Diablo. Here they were forced downstream a few miles to where precipitous walls fell away *(Wolf Crossing)*. Those without strict official permission to search for gold and silver were not likely to have left journals behind detailing their travels or what they found.

Coming up over the Mogollon Rim on the Navajo Trail, the train was attacked by an unknown tribe. Constant hit and run assaults forced the party west and north. They came in against Canyon Diablo somewhere around Two Guns. Standing off the Indians, the Spaniards followed downstream to where a crossing could be made.

According to a document and a map which came to light in 1902, the Spaniards were continually compelled to dispose of some of the weight overburdening the pack animals. Mules packing the silver were killed or gave out completely. The train gained part way along the side of Padre Canyon, which was so named for the fathers. Finally, against the Little Colorado, fatalities from Indian attack cut them down. As a final resort the many mule loads of silver bars were cached on the site of an abandoned Indian village.

Below is another photo taken of the breathtaking view of the Little Colorado River from the top off Padre Canyon that was taken by the author's friend Jeff Dunn and used with his permission. One can see by this picture how steepness and inaccessible of Canyon Diablo.

The survivors split apart, five attempting to escape west into California, and five headed east towards New Mexico. Apparently only the latter group made it through to their destination. For it was in the musty archives of the Old San Miguel mission in Santa Fe that the above-mentioned document was found.

The map locating the buried silver, and the account, brought many treasure hunters into the area. On one side of Padre Canyon, 18th century armor was recovered in 1919. One silver bar, approximately four- inches square, about twenty-three long and weighing 64 pounds, was found by a sheepherder. The discovery was made west of Two Guns in Bonito Park, and is believed to have been lost from a pack mule before the cache was made.

There is no question that there is a cache of gold and silver somewhere along the Little Colorado River somewhere near Padre Canyon. My friend Jeff Dunn has panned for gold along the river in the spring months and has found a lot of gold but the real cache is hidden somewhere along the river in a cave because it was not mined in that area. It was brought through the canyon by mule train.

Chapter Five

At this point the author would like to continue with the history of the town of Two Guns after the death of the Apache Raiding party. The Atlantic & Pacific Railroad passed through the area just four miles north of Two Guns and the Death Cave that lay underneath the town. What had previously been the route of the California-Santa Fe trail was hanged southward crossing Canyon Diablo just three miles north of the cave. From 1879 to just after the turn of the century a railroad town called Canyon Diablo was established while the railroad built the first bridge over the Canyon itself.

A serious earthquake at midnight on February 1, 1892 shook the entire plateau of northern Arizona. It collapsed the land bridge that was just to the north of the entrance to the cave at the bottom of Canyon Diablo. During the earthquake some of the fissures were filled with rocks and some massive rocks fell into the main cavern.

The Old Trails highway that would become US 66 crossed on a bridge built in 1913. It is now Interstate 40. In 1900 a couple were the first to stake claim to the 320 acres of land that included the town of Two Guns and of course the cave underneath but they only stayed a couple of years before they left suddenly for unknown reasons. Only a few outsiders knew about the cave but not how the crumbling human skeletal remains in the cave got there. Over the years wandering sheepherders, prospectors and treasure seekers carried away some of the skulls and bones from inside the cave.

In about 1907 several Flagstaff business firms decided that the road to Winslow could be shortened. West of the upper crossing they scraped out a flat road north to Two Guns. It passed down a long slope to the bottom of the canyon. On the east side, a dugway was blasted and torn through to the flat rim. During spring run off the canyon flooded deep. The short-cut crossing was then not useable, especially by the low-powered automobiles coming into general use. For that reason, the old Mormon crossing continued to be used by most travelers.

Mr. and Mrs. Daniel B. Oldfield, a childless couple in their fifties, settled in the area near Two Guns by the side of the new road. They built a square stone house, the ruins of that can be seen three miles south of Two Guns on the old road that is only a trail these days. In 1914 the road became known as the Old Trails Highway. Since then, it was called Route 66 and now it is Interstate 40, but the old road is still used along Interstate 40 and can be seen from the Interstate in several places.

In a small front room, the Oldfield's conducted a trading business with travelers, wandering prospectors, cowboys, sheepherders and Indians. Mr. and Mrs. Walter Drye entered Arizona in 1914 coming from Lee's Ferry on the Colorado River. A flat-bottomed barge was still employed for crossing transportation. After looking around, the Dry's selected a spot a mile above Two Guns. They built a rock house on the land they settled. The Dry's immediately went into the cattle business but they moved to nearby Anderson Mesa in 1929. The Dry relatives still live there today and they continue their parents endeavor, running a cattle business.

When the highway changed from upper Mormon Crossing to the crossing at Two Guns, an old time prospector, Ed Randolph started a business beside the section entering the canyon upstream from the Death Cave. When Earle and Louise Cundiff reached Arizona in 1922 from Arkansas, they paid Randolph $1,000 to relinquish his claim. Earle Cundiff was, a World War I army veteran, who proceeded to file a range claim of 320 acres, encompassing that part of the canyon now called Two Guns.

Cundiff constructed a large stone building complete with living quarters on the west side of the canyon where the dirt road turned down into the crossing. At a spot near his building down in the canyon he built a concrete dam to hold the river water, water being vital to his cattle operation and also to his family. As more and more automobiles came into general use, tourists began using the transcontinental highway *(Route 66)* across northern Arizona. From its beginning the trading post in its wonderful isolation enjoyed a good business.

The Cundiff's installed a gasoline tank, pumps, oil service, and a restaurant to take care of travelers. Harry E (Indian) Miller, claiming to be a full-blooded Apache Indian, and being part Mohawk, looked over possibilities at Two Guns. A well educated man possessing a flair for gaudy publicity, who served in the U.S. Army during the Spanish-American War, leased the business site from Cundiff for a period of ten years. In 1925, Miller called himself *"Chief Crazy Thunder,"* and wore his long hair braided and dressed as an Indian Chief.

After taking back the business from Miller, Cundiff and his wife began an extensive building program to take advantage of the large number of travelers to his business. On the canyon rim he put in a long stone structure the rear of which faced the main canyon, were wild animal cages and pens. He called this a lion farm (he had several mountain lions). The center of the building and entrance into the zoo contained a small store and living quarters.

Photos of Two Guns gas station and the lion zoo is in the background. This photo was taken at the time the Millers owned it. It is courtesy of the Arizona Historical Society.

Additional small buildings were also constructed on the premises, in which a restaurant and an Indian curio shop were owned by the Millers during the time they leased the property from the Cundiff's but it was operated by others. One of them was Hopi Chief Joe Secakuku. Investigating the Death Cave, thinking it would be another great attraction for travelers, Cundiff cleaned out the first two caverns. Cliff dweller ruins were then constructed inside the entry way and first cavern. What few Apache skulls he found were sold to tourists as souvenirs. The horse and human bones were disposed of to a Winslow bone dealer.

Below is a photo of the lion zoo and the Millers residence. This photo is courtesy of the Arizona Historical Society, Flagstaff branch.

Hopi Indians hired from their reservation built a pueblo type house on the side canyon rim directly over the cave. A paved path was built, connecting with a wooden bridge to a land island, and lookout points to a series of openings and eroded formations adjacent to the cave. For a nominal charge tourists were conducted through the Hopi house where fry bread was made and sold to tourists. In the cavern below a soft drink stand was installed, and electric wires run down through the first crack to provide lighting. During their first year or two living at their new home and business, the Miller's called the place *"Fort Two Guns."*

And eventually it was shortened to simply *"Two Guns."*

When Cundiff took the place back over he applied for a post office but his request was refused under that name. The designation *"Canyon Lodge,"* was accepted by the U.S. Post office. Cundiff then became official postmaster, when it opened for business in his store at the bridge, November 24, 1924. Begun in late 1925, completed in 1926, the state rerouted the highway past the Cundiff store directly in front, and built a concrete bridge. This old road made a sharp right turn off the bridge, passing before the elaborately signed Hopi house.

From the beginning arguments ensued between Cundiff and Miller over the latter's assumption of extra rights under rather broad terms of his lease. Unfortunately Cundiff did not listen to the Navajo Indians who worked for him, who had warned him that Miller was a dangerous man. The crisis came the evening of March 3, 1926, when Miller shot Cundiff to death. The body had been dragged out of Miller's living quarters at the zoo when county officers arrived to investigate.

Following the formalities of a trial and despite the fact that Cundiff had been unarmed, Miller was acquitted of the charge of murder. The interior of the big store burned out in the fall of 1929. Mrs. Cundiff built a large frame building from which she continued to conduct a trading post and tourist stop, east of the bridge and north in the red clay flats.

When she arranged to improve up on the homestead, Miller filed protests. He said that the land was rightly his and that he was actually there before the Cundiffs.

After Cundiff's death Miller constructed a sprawling zoo and buildings on Canyon Diablo's rim. He hired Hopi Indians to clean out the bones from the cave. Neither the Navajos or Apaches would have anything to do with the cave but the Hopi's agreed to clean out the cave for Miller. After they finished cleaning out the cave, Miller strung wires from an electric plant and made it into a tourist attraction.

Knowing nothing of the death fight that took place in the cave, he used the remaining human bones to add stage-dressing to all the pseudo-ancient aboriginal ruins he created inside the cave and the canyon itself. He then called it the Mystery Cave.

For the next ten years Harry Miller experienced nothing but bad luck. He was charged with killing Cundiff. The authorities were not able to provide enough evidence to get a conviction so Miller was found not guilty of the murder of Cundiff. Shortly after he was released a Hopi Indian that was working for him died under mysterious circumstances.

A few months after the Hopi workman passed away, a caged cougar attacked and seriously injured Miller during a feeding operation. A year later a lynx cat so severely clawed him that he spent six months in a hospital while his body healed from the near death experience. If that was not bad enough to make a person wonder, his seventeen-year old beautiful daughter died in a highway accident near the bridge that spanned the Canyon.

The nearby Navajos again warned Miller that the canyon over which Cundiff built the town named Two Guns, was a place were evil spirits wandered at will. Mysterious groans, noises and heavy footsteps of walking men were often heard at night. Awakened from sound sleep, Two Guns dwellers often rushed outside but saw nothing either living or ghostly.

Miller's lease on his part at Two Guns was a source of constant tribulation to him. In his zoo was every beast and bird native to Arizona, from tiny coral snakes to cougars.

One of the mountain lions clawed him almost to death. A year later a small Canada lynx very nearly disemboweled him. Another time a Gila monster on exhibit as an attraction before the zoo entrance, clamped toothless jaws fast to a right finger. The wound infected, his arm swelling enormously to the shoulder. Six months elapsed before it became normal again.

He also had domestic troubles. Then someone maliciously ripped down all his flamboyant advertising signs along the highway. In court, he charged six different people with the deed. One of them was found guilty in court and fined $90. Through a series of court actions that cost her $15,000 Mrs. Cundiff over a ten year period, finally cleared the title. The government patent was received in July, 1929, and signed by President Herbert Hoover.

With all the trouble suffered, along with now not even being the owner, Miller had made up his mind to leave Two Guns. The climax came in a very badly hushed-up case, the details not remembered by local people today. He left the State a year after Mrs. Cundiff obtained clear ownership in 1930 to avoid prosecution on many serious charges.

Crossing the Arizona line into New Mexico, he put in a similar zoo and tourist attraction north of Highway 66. As before, he constructed phony cliff dweller's ruins, where none had ever existed, in a cave in a sandstone cliff wall. The name *"Cave of the Seven Devils,"* was painted in huge letters over the cave, and visible from the highway. He lived there until his death in February, 1952.

After Miller's departure, Mrs. Cundiff leased the Two Guns buildings to various people. Earl Tinning of Flagstaff managed the business and ran a restaurant from 1933 to the end of 1935. Phillip E. Hesch, Santa Fe Railroad signal maintainer at Canyon Diablo station, and the widow Cundiff were married December 9, 1934. That year the big trading post at Canyon Diablo burned to the ground. Hesch rescued Depot Agent Rowan from the flaming building barely in the nick of time.

That same year Mrs. Ray Thomas, with an invalid husband, taught school at Canyon Diablo station. Obtaining a permit, she began constructing a red sandstone home with a flat roof, directly below the Hopi house. She planned to live there with her husband but he had to be confined in an insane asylum and it was never finished. After Tinning's lease expired the Hesch's took over the Two Guns property to manage it themselves.

The last rerouting of Highway 66 occurred in 1938, still crossing Two Guns land. A new bridge was built over Canyon Diablo downstream from the first one. Hesch moved two frame buildings to the new highway side. They had a store, along with gasoline pumps, a restaurant and living quarters in the back of the store. The zoo and lion farm were re-established by Hesch, was located a few yards behind their living quarters that had been built on the edge of the canyon walls by Miller.

The transcontinental highway took on the curse of evil very early. Even before automobile traffic grew heavy, the roads around Two Guns exacted a heavy toll of lives. While still a mere dirt road, a few of the skulls from the cave were posted on rock pyramids beside it as a warning to drivers to be careful. Today those skulls have been replaced by small white crosses to indicate a place where people lost their lives in auto accidents.

The ruined buildings of old Two Guns are visible for many miles. Tourists stop to photograph them. A few venture down a precarious wall to look inside the Death Cave, not knowing its history or what happened there in the cave over one hundred years ago. Only occasionally does anyone enter the forbidding cavern where the cold air remains the same temperature they year around.

Benjamin F. Dreher, who bought the Two Guns in the 1960's and was only half heartedly willing to discuss his plans to clean it out and restore it for the possibility of allowing visitors to enter the cave. It is the longest and most attractive cavern in Arizona. Even though he knew its history, Dreher was not deterred by the alleged spirits of the dead inhabiting the cave that the Navajo had warned him about.

He hired nearby Hopi villagers to clean out the cave for him then he went ahead and had them build up the inside of the caverns to look like ceremonial places. He opened the cave to the public but a lot of weird things happened to him and after he passed away the cave was left alone.

Chapter Six

Peaceful Indians living around Newberry and Garces Mesas, Navajo villages that were located a few miles north of Wolf Crossing and Trading Post on the Little Colorado River on the southern border of the Navajo Reservation, woke up to a cold morning early in the month of June in the year 1878. In that early morning dawn, a coyote babbled, hardly unusual, but with it was answered by a gobbling turkey, a sign the doomed Navajo's knew was the worst.

The men grabbed weapons and rushed out to defend their village and their families. But they were too late. A hated Apache raiding party from the south had already closed in around the village. Gun explosions ripped the morning air. A few arrows feathered swiftly into human targets. Shrieking war cries of death, dusky Apache warriors charged five the community Hogan's.

Within minutes that bloody June dawn, 1878, all the men, women and children, except three young girls taken prisoners, were slain. Robbing the dead and pilfering Hogan's for loot, the band of twenty raiders disappeared into the wastelands where their horses had been hidden from the sight of the villagers.

A second raiding party struck a Hogan cluster on the west side of Newberry Mesa, just north of Wolf Trading Post and Crossing on the Little Colorado River, that same June morning. They followed the same procedure, killing almost all of the residents of the village but they vanished not taking any captives or horses but only tradable loot and food.

The Navajo were stunned by the swiftness of the raids. District leaders, Bugoettin Begay, Natani and Chief Hosteen Redshirt immediately gathered to discuss how they would handle the problem. It was obvious that the Apaches were not going to go away easily. They feared the possibility of more raids. The Navajo in general were farmers and raised stock. Navajo pottery, blankets and jewelry were valued tradable items to the Apaches. The Navajo were not all farmers and ranchers. They also had an elite group of braves that would have been similar to our U.S. Marine Green Berets, so the area chiefs put out a call to arms and twenty-five fighting men gathered by the next morning. The Navajo hunting party, after gathering supplies headed south down the Little Colorado River Basin, the long deep, winding Canyon Diablo. They hoped to cut off the raiders in flight.

Seldom did the Navajo enemies cross the Little Colorado River at Wolf Trading Post.

When questioned by the Navajo Chiefs', Herman Wolf, the only white man living in the area, a trader and friend to the Navajo, told them he heard the raiding party go past his trading post in the middle of the night. He said he had the post locked down but he figured the Apaches probably did not see his building in the dark of the night. Wolf told the chiefs that he saw them later that same morning coming back by the post on their way south but that they were in a hurry. He told the chiefs that he saw the three captive women with them as they rode by his trading post.

The Navajo hunting party lurked in the Mogollon Rim trails for two days searching for the Apache raiding parties. But they could find no sign of the plight of the raiding parties. Puzzled at the fact that their enemies seemed to disappear into thin air, they started homeward the next day. A messenger in route gave them delivered the tragic news. The enemy again raided over the river, that same morning.

In this raid more than thirty Navajo were killed. This time a wounded brave survived. He recognized the Apache leader, known to them as *"Crooked Jaw."* It was Naiche, for sure, the son of Cochise the famed Chiricahuan chief, who after the death of his brother Tarza, became the leader of the

Chirichua tribe, who were living at the San Carlos Apache Reservation east of Globe, Arizona.

Enraged by the sneak attack and murder of innocent people, the three Navajo area chiefs, Natani, Bugoettin Begay, and Hosteen Redshirt called for vengeance and organized twenty-five fighting braves, fearing for more attacks immediately set out south of the Little Colorado river hoping to catch their enemies and end their existence. They figured their enemies would return to the Mogollon Rim trails, from which they simply must have had to have come. Redshirt led four scouts east in a half circle, and Natani led another party west. Bugoetin Begay followed the trail through Canyon Diablo along the Little Colorado River basin. They planned to meet at the Mogollon Trail. They figured that in separating they would have a better chance of getting ahead of their enemy and possible cut them off somewhere along the way. They hoped to pick up the Apache escaping signs but their enemy seemed to disappear into thin air.

Not finding their enemy, fearing there might be a third bloody dawn attack by the Apache raiding party, the Navajo leaders returned to the river at Wolf Crossing which is the only place along Canyon Diablo that the river can be crossed, they arrived by midnight. Their scouts hid in the timber that was growing all along the banks of the stream. But no Apache raiding parties came to invade across the Little Colorado into Navajo country. The next morning the three chiefs sent scouts south again to look for sign of their enemies but they found no trace of the enemy anywhere from Wolf Crossing as far south as the trails along the Mogollon Rim, some fifty miles south of Wolf Crossing.

Two things puzzled the Navajo leaders, failure of the enemy to take horses and their successful vanishing act. After re-crossing the river heading south the two raiding parties had split into small groups, their trails disappearing into the malapais and the cinder bed country near the remains of the meteor crater.

As the three chiefs sat around in council by a campfire on the other side of the river from Wolf Post that night while they waited for their enemy to show their faces again, Chief Natani declared;

"They did not go away,"

While they waited for their enemy to strike again, they had a real surprise for the raiding parties if they came back for more raids.

Finally, he looked at the rest of the chiefs and said;

> "They have a hiding place. From it they will raid again before streaking south to their own homeland or back on the reservation."

At that point the chiefs agreed that the three young girls that were taken from their village were quickly tortured to death for the enemy's sadistic amusement. But this also posed another question: Navajo scouts had roved the area below the Little Colorado River basin and the Canyon Diablo area. The screams from the tortured prisoners would have echoed over considerable distance. Yet the scouts heard nothing while out looking for their enemies. Finally, Chief Begay figured them out and declared allowed;

> "They are in the ground somewhere between the river and the Mogollon Rim Trails. It is how they have escaped detection and it must be close enough to allow them to perform surprise raids and then disappear."

This logic was highly possible, for several wide and deep volcanic cracks and lava tubes radiated out from the distant San Francisco Peaks, sleeping volcanoes that at one time earlier in time were live volcanoes that created the mountains. The next morning scouts were sent to five of the most likely spots that contained large caves or lava tubes that could be used as hiding places. The scouts returned later that day stating that they could find no evidence of the wily Apaches.

Chief Bugoetten Begay along with one scout was dispatched fifteen miles to the south of the river to inspect a cave in the two hundred fifty-foot deep Canyon Diablo, Little Colorado River basin underneath what eventually would become the ghost town of "Two Guns."

On the mere possibility they could be there, Chief Begay himself and a scout by the name of Bahe left their horses on Long Canyon, a side canyon that led into the main Canyon Diablo. When interviewed by Maurice Kildare some fifty years later, he remembered the whole ordeal like it was yesterday;

> *"We started crawling on our hands and knees through the tall grass and sagebrush toward the rim of Canyon Diablo so that we would surprise our enemies if in fact they were hiding in the cave at the bottom of the Canyon."*

He went on to say;

> "Within a minute or so while crawling just before the edge of the canyon we encountered a very creepy situation. All at once voices sounded before our faces. They came at us from out of the ground. We thought for sure evil spirits were talking to us. In a way they were living dead men!"

But in fact the voices were those of Apaches, and next, they felt fire generated heat against their faces. Crawling a yard further toward the rim they detected reflected light in the ground between clumps of sagebrush. Calming their badly shaken nerves, the young strapping Chief, Bugoettin Begay and the scout Bahe gathered their thoughts as they looked at each other realizing that it was an eight-inch narrow crack in the ground straight down through solid stone that went into an underground cavern. It was then they realized the Apaches and their mounts were hiding somewhere in the cave right below them. After gathering their thoughts, they decided reluctantly to get back to the rest of the hunting party so they could make plans. At this point they were undetected by the enemy and they would not move since they felt they were in the safety of their hiding place so Begay and Bahe felt, there enemies were not going be leaving anytime soon.

Chief's Bugoettin Begay, Natani and Redshirt were probably the wiliest of desert guerrilla strategists. Just because the Navajo were known as ranchers and farmers, don't be fooled that they did not know how or have superior fighters amidst their people. If their enemy thought they could get away with attacking innocent villages and get away with it, they would be sadly mistaken. The plan was simple; they were going to wipeout the raiders to the last man. They wanted to exact vengeance from their enemies for the horrible atrocities they had committed on their three villages and their innocent relatives that lived in those villages. They spent that evening dancing around the campfire preparing their plans for killing their enemies.

Below are photos of the three Navajo Chiefs that were taken later in their lives.

Bugoettin Begay   Natani   Redshirt

Knowing the situation and the fact that the Apaches would actually be trapped in their secure hiding place, Redshirt and Natani, along with ten fighting men followed Bugoettin Begay and Bahe as they led the hunting party to the edge of the Canyon. The mouth of the cave was located inside a wall of a side canyon in the floor of the 250-foot deep Canyon Diablo underneath what is now left of the ghost town of *"Two Guns."*

They waited at the edge of the canyon in concealment for nightfall. After it descended and when the moon rose, Chief Redshirt and his braves rode openly to the canyon rim, deliberately silhouetting them against the domed night sky. The cave was concealed by fallen large blocks of stone. It was difficult to locate in the dark but luckily Begay and Bahe remembered exactly where it was located. A few yards from the narrow entrance was a land bridge, with a massive rock island just to the north of the entrance to the cave. There was also a fallen wooden ladder that partly covered the entrance.

The trail to the cave entrance passed under the land bridge. A pony could barely squeeze through. But once inside the narrow entrance was a wide passageway swinging right for seventy feet, then the cave made a left turn into the first large cavern. It along with the nearby second cavern provided ample space for the raiders and their mounts. Beyond them were several other large caverns, which since have been explored and continue for more than four miles underground.

Having revealed them selves as ostensibly as possible, the Navajo hunting party withdrew by riding south along the rim. Behind them Bugoetten and Baha were concealed in the rocks, peering over into the mouth of the cave. When the party with Redshirt and Natani had disappeared from the view, two Apache guards revealed themselves incautiously. One dropped of the wall directly below where Bugoetten Begay and Baha were hiding. The second Apache showed from the opposite side of the entrance to the cave. They both hurried into the cave. The Apaches reacted just as Redshirt, Natani and Begay planned. Redshirt and his braves moved from around the corner from where they were hiding on foot and surrounded the mouth of the cave.

Chief Begay and Bahe concealed themselves behind brush and rock closing off the entrance and any possible avenue of escape. As they set themselves up in strategic positions they could hear the sounds of their enemy's ponies moving around in the cave.

There was evidence of grazed off grass that showed that the Apache stock had been out in the side canyon during daylight hours grazing.

While Begay and Baha guarded the mouth of the cave, Redshirt, Natani and the other braves gathered dead wood and highly inflammable dry brush. The plan was to smoke the Apaches out or suffocate them in the cave. While these preparations were under way, two Apache braves emerged from the entrance of the cave. They were immediately shot and killed. This was the first warning to the Apaches that they were trapped in their hiding place and were completely surrounded.

Gunfire came from inside the cave from the Apaches hit the rocky walls of the opposite side of the canyon near where the two guards were posted, but since the enemy had a limited view of their enemy, they followed the gunfire by a feeble charge from out of the mouth of the cave. The attempted escape failed because there wasn't enough room to maneuver in the confines of the entrance of the cave and with fire coming from the Navajos the enemy was forced back inside the cave. The trapped Apaches kept up steady pointless barrages of gunfire but again there was no way they could see anyone outside the cave to hit.

The Navajos on guard returned fire to keep the enemy cooped up. The wood and brush was piled up on the rim over the entrance to the cave some forty feet below and set on fire. When the mass blazed furiously it was shoved over the edge of the mesa and it fell directly over the entrance to the cave. Two braves ran out of the cave and shoved the flaming pile away so the draft would not suck fumes into the cave. They were killed and their bodies partly blocked the cave entrance,

Realizing what the Navajos were up to, the Apaches grew desperate. Again two more braves tried another sortie and again they were killed in their tracks with their bodies now lying in the entrance with the other two that were killed in the earlier attempt. The other Apaches still in the cave managed to get back inside to safety through the leaping flames. Some were seen on fire with their clothing in flames.

As it appeared the Apaches would somehow prevent the mass of flames from sucking into the cave, Chief Redshirt proposed filling the tunnel-like passage solid with stones dropping them from the rim above the entrance to the cave. The young Chief, Bugoettin Begay, immediately opposed the idea stating;

> *"One of my married daughters, her husband and all of their children were slain on the first morning raid under the red walled Garces Mesa. I do not want to take a chance that they might escape. I want them all dead when we leave this place."*

A second mass of burning wood and brush was thrust away from the entrance. It was then Chief Begay changed strategy slightly. While the brush burned furiously more material was gathered and piled on the land bridge. A large heap also decorated the rim over the entrance to the cave. Both piles were set on fire and dumped over, completely filling the passageway higher than a man's head.

The fumes and smoke were sucked inside the cave. Up out of the ground on the plateau under which the cave lay, smoke streamed into the night sky, not form one fissure, but three other fissures. It looked like the desired end for the Apache raiding party. Then, spreading smoke against the stars and moonlight began to die out. The fumes no longer entered the cavern. A Navajo on the rim started into the abyss below. He discovered the last desperate attempt of the Apaches to save them selves. They found some water containers as well as what they realized later was blood from cut ponies throats that they threw into the flames in the mouth of the cave to try to extinguish the fire. They also piled up stones into the entrance behind the flames hoping to block the flames and fumes from entering the depths of the cave. The Navajo scout could hear voices from deeper in the cave so he ran out of the cave yelling to Begay, Redshirt and Natani that some of the enemy raiders were still alive and hiding deeper in the cave.

It was decided by the three chiefs that one final attempt to burn them out would finish the job. All flammable material close at hand had been exhausted. It was now necessary to go farther away for more material. Most of what was gathered was sagebrush pulled out of the ground. Two more huge piles were collected and placed in the mouth of the cave.

During this delay the raiders made one last attempt to escape from the cave. Rushing out they leaped upward on the loose rocks, trying to scale the perpendicular wall above the cave to the ledges above. As they popped into the moonlight, rifle fire from the Navajos dropped them dead and their bodies fell back down in front of the entrance to the cave.

By then there was a ten-foot long space of smoldering embers directly before the entrance to the cave. Behind the protection of a stone shoulder an Apache speaking broken Navajo hailed the besiegers;

> "We need not fight this way. Where is Crooked Jaw?"

Chief Natani demanded;

> "We will only listen on to your leader. What happened to him?"

Declared Natani;

> "He went south this afternoon with two other braves. He was summoned home for a family emergency."

Said the raiding brave who seemed to be in charge, or at least who was the spokesmen for the Apaches. Sadly, the hated raiding leader, Naiche escaped Navajo vengeance by running away. Natani ordered;

> "Send out the three girls you took as captives?"

The spokesman hesitated a long time. His delay confirmed what the Navajo Chief's already believed. The hapless prisoners had been put to cruel death the first day of the raid. Finally, the spokesman declared;

> "We took no captives. I do not know why you accuse us of this."

Chief Natani spoke sternly;

> "You can escape death by fire, if you come out five at a time. Stand in front of the rocks and there we will execute you for the wrongs you have committed. Wait, I must discuss this with the others!"

Said the trapped Apache brave who seemed to be the spokesman for the raiding party in their chief's absence. Chief Natani immediately shouted;

> "There will be no waiting for you. All must die!"

The Apache raider's stalling attempts were not tolerated. From the rim above the land bridge masses of more flammable sagebrush was heaved into the deep passage. It was filled with an overflow reaching to the rock strewn ledges above the entrance to the cave.

Smoke again poured out of the earth cracks into the night sky. The screams from the Apache raiding party could be heard along with the shirking sounds of frightened ponies echoing. Followed by the blood curdling shrieks of the doomed raiders, their death chants added to the fearful grotesque situation. It appeared that abandoning all hope, the enemy prepared to die the hard way.

The Navajo warriors began yelling their victory chant, but their exultation proved a little premature. After nearly an hour the smoke ensuing from the fissures above the cave on the mesa began to dwindle until only a few tendrils wafted skyward.

At that point the Navajos armed for further fighting entered the cave to inspect the holocaust of hell that filled the entrance to the cave. Added to the conflagration was the stench of what they presumed to be burning bodies. Later they were to find out that most of nauseating odor came from the pieces of pony carcasses. Their mounts that had been throat-cut earlier were quartered and the chunks of flesh crammed solid into the cave mouth as a barrier to keep out the fumes. These acts in desperation constituted the Apache raiders' final attempt to save themselves.

But they failed, for two possible reasons. Not many remained alive strong enough to build the flesh barricade all the way to the overhead, or else they couldn't reach it. The Navajo poured on more brush. Watching anxiously for smoke to come out of the fissures again, slowly the horrible screams and chants below died away to eternal silence. By then the smoke once more ensued from the fissures, although not in great volume until almost an hour later.

Smoke again poured out of the earth cracks into the night sky. The sound of screaming frightened pony sounds echoing with it. Followed by the blood curdling shrieks of the doomed raiders, their death chants added to the fearful grotesque situation. It appeared that abandoning all hope, the enemy prepared to die the hard way.

The Navajo braves again began yelling their victory chant. But their exultation proved a little premature. After nearly an hour the smoke ensuing from the fissures above the cave on the mesa began to dwindle until only a few tendrils wafted skyward.

The photo on the next page is of the entrance to the Death Cave that was used by the author for the cover of this book. This photo was also taken by the author's friend Jeff Dunn. It shows the entrance to the cave that is under the wood bridge and the ledges above the cave from where the burning brush was dropped. One can see how futile it was for the trapped Apaches to try to scale the sides of the ledges in an attempt to escape their burning fate and made a perfect target for the Navajos that were positioned right across from the entrance to the cave.

When the fierce fire burned down to a hot pit Natani said it wasn't necessary to add anymore fuel to the fire. Chief Natani declared in a loud and clear voice;

> "The enemy is gone, our work is finished here. Let it be so," he declared to all present."

Indeed at this point their revenge had been consummated. The sun came up that morning with a red ring on the horizon. The great fire became ashes and fading embers. The side walls of the stone were too hot to touch until they cooled off. The Navajos sat on the upper ledges waiting in silence. A rising wind whipped ashes away from the entrance to the cave. It was then they spotted the solid mass of roasted pony meat the covered the opening of the cave.

By mid morning a few men were able to stand in the uncovered tunnel below. They cleaned away the ten feet of pony pieces and human bones, stones and stray glowing embers. Using poles, they punched out the burned pony flesh so as to get a clearing draft of air into the cave. Fumes still clinging in the grottos and caverns could be deadly.

When noon arrived that cloudy day, before the scouts ventured inside the cave, the passageway breaking right contained no dead enemy bodies. But upon reaching the small side pockets the scouts found a few bodies contorted from death throes. Torches of gummy wood were necessary to provide light as it was as dark as a moonless night in the cave.

The first large cavern revealed a macabre scene of death. It was literally crammed with the carcasses of dead ponies and Apaches. Most of the enemy lay dead on a stone platform above the ponies. At the low, narrow entrance into the second cavern, they came upon another chilling scene.

Several ponies had tried to get through to breathing space in the second cavern. Their bodies blocked it. The Apache pulled them aside barely enough to crawl through a small hole. Then apparently in panic too many rushed in an attempt to escape their impending doom. Their bodies were pulled out of the way and the Navajo braves as they entered another silent tomb of death. Only five Apache bodies were found in that cavern. In the hot stream of air found in that cavern, lying around, twisted in death were their bodies, where they died gulping for the non-existent oxygen.

The third cavern was checked, but the six inches of rock dust covering the floor had not been disturbed. None of those caught in the cave had escaped. Fifty-four dead Apaches were counted by the Navajo scouts. A hunt was made for the bodies of the three girls that were taken as captives. They were never found, inside or outside the cave. Presumably they had been dropped into one of the several bottomless fissures.

Below is a photo taken in the early 1880's found in our National Archives is of a typical Apache raiding party.

The enemy's bodies were stripped of firearms and anything else of value. The items that were taken from the Navajo villages were recovered before the victorious tribesmen withdrew. They came out quietly, awed by the awful toll they exacted. But none felt any pity for the cruel enemy murderers. The spirits of their own recent dead wept for atonement. In the dusk the non-talking group of Navajo braves dismounted at Wolf Post on the Little Colorado River. Entering the post, they smoked the free tobacco, and at last in awed and wondering gutturals, told their story to Herman Wolf, their friend, the white trader with whom they traded goods for several years. Wolf told them that he felt very lucky that the raiding party was in a hurry as they came back by the morning of the massacre they inflicted on the sleeping nearby Navajo village, or for sure if they had not been in a hurry, they would have raided his store and killed everyone.

When and how the news of the awful disaster to the Apache raiders reached the San Carlos Apache Reservation was never discovered, but it did. From that point on, when venturing onto the great northern plateau, raiding Apaches that jumped the reservation avoided that part of Canyon Diablo as cursed by spirits where ghosts abided. Indeed, all Indians shunned the cave, known as a place of danger and horror. It gained an evil name among all the Indian Nations and numerous legends sprung up about its awesome secret of the dead Apaches.

In fact, it has been over a hundred and thirty years since the raiding Apache braves were slaughtered and there has never been the sign of any life form found in the cave except for bats. Not an animal of any kind has ever been seen or left any droppings in the cave.

Below is a painting of an Apache Raiding party that was found on the Pinterest Website that was painted by an unknown artist and is public domain the author used for the cover of this book.

Chapter Seven

Onyx became a valuable commodity in the mid 1890's for use in architecture, the making of table tops and Onyx jewelry. It could be found in a number of canyons south of the Little Colorado. Prospectors staked claims and mining started to boom. But only briefly, for enough of the onyx ore was discovered in Grapevine and Deer Canyons above Two Guns to supply the entire domestic demand for many years. It was shipped to Los Angeles to Chicago and New York on the east coast. It was hauled out of the steep canyons in two-wheeled or one-horse carts. When the Spanish-American War erupted in 1898, the Flagstaff Blues, a local uniformed militia, was formed as happened in many other southwestern towns. Their first action was to chase down and pursue a murderer who killed an Indian woman in a cabin across the canyon east of Two Guns.

Then again in the next year 1899, the Flagstaff Blues were called out to put down a Navajo uprising in the vicinity of Canyon Diablo station. Hardly was that done, without bloodshed, when a band of stock thieves holed up in the gorge a mile upstream from Two Guns. When their hiding place was discovered the gang numbered about fifteen. In addition to Arizona, the outlaws were wanted in Utah and New Mexico. Riding at night in their dashing uniforms, the Flagstaff Blues surrounded their camp and captured the entire bunch without firing a shot. From the first years of encroachment on their ancestral lands by white stockmen around Two Guns and to the Little Colorado, the Navajo protested in vain. But when footloose cowboys began running off their horses they took punitive action. At first, when caught, cowboy thieves were roughed up but not killed.

One cowboy, who arrived near the canyon in 1884, soon earned their deepest hatred. He was accused not only of rustling their stock, especially their cattle, but when his roundup wagons moved camp, of leaving arsenic behind in baking powder tins mixed with a remnant. Women scavenged these camps, picking up cast-away articles that might be of use to them. They collected the poisoned baking powder into one can. Used to make bread, one entire family of seven was wiped out. For awhile, unable to get an ambush shot at the cowboy, they damaged him in another way. When any of his cattle were found bogged down in the river quicksand, enough green hide was cut off the live animal to sew a pair of moccasins.

After a few distant shots were taken at him the cowman feared for his life. Yet he remained contemptuous of what the Navajo could do. Then one day while riding the river with another man, a single bullet whined at him. Missing him by a mere whisper, it killed the rider at his side. Soon after that the cowman sold out and retired to the safety of Flagstaff.

In another skirmish a cowboy named William Montgomery was accosted by three Navajo braves near some of their ponies. They proceeded to administer a good beating. Going to Flagstaff he swore to warrants charging aggravated assault and battery. Deputy Sheriff Dan Hogan was sent back with Montgomery to serve the warrants. Stopping at the Roden cowboy camp, Roden and Walter Durham were added to the posse.

The four men rode to the rim of Elliott Canyon, near the junction of Padre and Diablo Canyons downstream from Two Guns. Locating a Navajo camp in the brush below in the late afternoon of November 8, 1899, they dismounted and walked down. They slipped up on a brush shelter and halted. Leaning over to peer inside, Hogan saw an old man tanning a buckskin hide. Unseen in the brush nearby lurked armed Navajos.

The sight of the horse thief Montgomery triggered them into action. Suddenly a blast of gunfire spewed into the white men. Hogan was wounded by a long gash across the shoulders while bent over. Montgomery was killed instantly. Deputy Sheriff Roden was shot through the groin. As the men began withdrawing, they poured lead into the shelter, killing the unarmed, harmless old man. It was then near sundown. The three survivors dared not climb the exposed canyon wall to their saddled horses. Fleeing through the brush, they walked all night, lost and wandering around, to the railroad. Durham had to pack Roden most of the way.

At dawn they caught a freight train to Flagstaff where the shooting scrape was reported. Alarm spread through the area. But more scared were the Navajo. They felt sure that military or the Flagstaff Blues militia would be sent to round them up by force. Once more families sought refuge in Canyon Diablo. The countryside remained in turmoil for three weeks before government agents could take a hand adjudicating the controversy. The Navajo involved were told to report in Flagstaff for a hearing.

This they refused to do at first. Finally, one night, 300 heavily armed Navajo braves led by aging Chief Bugoettin Begay, a veteran of so many fights with the Apache, stopped at Wolf Post on the river. At that time S. I. Richardson was the resident trader. With his uncle, George W. McAdams, he had purchased the post in 1899 after Wolf's death. They informed Begay that white men were making war on them. Once before the soldiers had come to fight them, at that time the Navajo were imprisoned them at Fort Sumner. This time they would wipe out the town of Flagstaff! They could easily have done this for the small, unprotected town had less than a thousand inhabitants.

Then surprisingly, after war-like statements, Chief Bugoettin Begay asked Richardson what he thought would happen if those concerned surrendered for the hearing;

> "You will be turned loose by the judge."

He replied.

> "The white men were in the wrong and you can prove it."

The war party rode on without revealing what they would really do. Passing up the near side of Canyon Diablo they cut west from Two Guns to concealment in thick standing pine timber, approaching the town of Flagstaff from an unexpected direction.

Three days later they were back at Wolf Trading Post, laughing and talking about what had happened. The large party hid in the timber within quick striking distance. Three men, one of them Chief Begay, went in unarmed, taking the four horses and saddles seized by them after the shooting fray. Their plan was that if the three were jailed, the war party would strike in the dead of night, burn down the town and kill all who opposed them. Fortunately, the judge before whom the hearing was held found insufficient evidence to hold anyone accountable for the deaths of the three men, thus ending any further interaction between the Navajo and the town of Flagstaff.

Chapter Eight

We are now going to go to the year 1886, when Fred Volz established an Indian trading post in railroad town of Canyon Diablo, which was located on the southwestern boundary of the Navajo reservation, only three miles north of Two Guns.

Volz and his wife stayed on until 1910, and played a role in documenting one of the most bizarre shootouts ever to take place in the West. This shootout lasted all of three seconds, as compared to Tombstone's famous gunfight at the OK Corral, which lasted around 30 seconds. All four combatants within site of Two Guns emptied their six-guns in what eyewitnesses described as *"a single explosion."*

In the year 1905, beginning on the night of April 7, there occurred one of the most bizarre incidents in western history, ending within sight of Two Guns. Two cowboys, John Shaw and Bill Smith, twenty-two and twenty-four years old, entered the Wigwam Saloon on Second Street in Winslow.

Upon ordering a drink, and while the bartender poured, their eyes bugged out at sight of between 400 and 600 silver dollars stacked on the dice table run by Frank

Ketchum, cousin to the famous New Mexico train robbers Thomas Blackjack Ketchum and Sam Ketchum. Glancing quickly at Shaw, Smith nodded his head in a signal. Out of their holsters came their pistols and holding the men at the table at bay they stuffed the Silver dollars into all their pockets and when their pockets were filled they put the rest in their hats. Then they backed out and made good temporary escape.

Navajo County Deputy Sheriff Pete Pemberton was immediately notified. He, in turn, wired Navajo County Sheriff Chet Houck *(younger brother of J.D. Houck of Pleasant Valley War fame)* in Holbrook. Pemberton and Winslow City Marshal Bob Giles found a trail of silver coins leading to the train tracks, and they assumed the robbers had hopped the westbound train to Flagstaff. Houck and Pemberton boarded the next train to Flagstaff, hoping to join in the search now going on for the two robbers. No trace of them could be found in Flagstaff, so the lawman took the next train back to Winslow on the afternoon of April 8, 1905.

While on the trip back, they learned that two men had been seen hiding in the brush near the right-of-way to Canyon Diablo. Stopping the train, a couple of miles past Canyon Diablo, Houck and Pemberton went back toward the town on foot. The sun was just setting over the distant San Francisco Peaks when they reached Canyon Diablo.

There they met Fred Volz, former railroad telegrapher turned Indian trader to the Navajos and Hopis. Volz told Houck and Pemberton that he had noticed two suspicious-looking characters hanging around the trading post all day. At that moment, Houck and Pemberton spotted the two men and approached them after they rounded a building. As they came within six to eight feet of one another, the two lawmen asked to search them. One of the outlaws responded;

"No one searches us!"

Immediately, all four men jerked their six-guns and began to firing in rapid succession. In the bat of an eye a gunfight erupted. Twenty shots were fired during which Houck's clothing was holed several times and Smith was wounded. Customarily that many cartridges would have been loaded in only four guns, the firing pin resting on the sixth, the empty chamber. Only Pemberton did not observe this safety precaution. He had six bullets loaded and the last one brought Shaw down dead as he wheeled to flee with an empty gun.

Shaw was hurriedly buried that night and Smith removed to the Winslow hospital. Over in the Wigwam Saloon a bunch of liquoring cowboys heard the story of the shoot-out, which had been telephoned from Canyon Diablo. Out of a long stretch of silence one of them remarked seriously;

> "Them two boys paid for drinks and didn't down their whiskey. Was Shaw given a snort before they planted him?"

Another replied sarcastically;

> "Now, you know lawmen don't go around giving a dead man no drink! Shucks, our friend has a drink coming to him and not getting what he paid for ain't right. We should go to Canyon Diablo and give him one!"

The idea caught on quickly and within twenty-minutes, fifteen drunken Hash knife cowboys, each with a bottle of whiskey in hand, hitched a ride on the Santa Fe back to Canyon Diablo. Arriving there around dawn, they woke up Fred Volz, who gave them some shovels and a Kodak camera. While digging up Shaw and hauling him out of his coffin to pour his last drink, the cowboys noticed a slight smile on his face. This was enough to wipe the smiles from their faces and dissipate their own hilarity.

The countenance of John Shaw brought tears to many of the onlooker's eyes. Affected the most was the Hash knife cowboy, many of whom was his acquaintances and also was on the run from the law in Texas and using assumed names. They probably saw their own wild past reflected in the blank eyes staring from the coffin.

Shaw was then given several going-away drinks from the bottles the fifteen men brought with them as the new sun cleared the horizon. There was enough light to snap pictures before Shaw was replanted.

As Shaw was replanted with the half-empty bottle of whiskey, the cowboys stood around with their hats off. After the macabre lasted several hours, the cowboys eventually sobered up, realizing what they had done, they left quietly.

Two of those original brutal photographs of the late John Shaw are pictured below as he is being prepared to receive *"a large gulp of whiskey"* from the Hash knife cowboys.

On the next page are photos below of John Shaw's fate are courtesy of the

Arizona Historical Society, the Flagstaff Arizona Branch

Today, nothing much is left of the town of canyon Diablo but fragments of buildings and heaps of silent stones to mark what was once a town named after and owned by the devil.

Below is a photo of the Canyon Diablo Trading Post that was taken in 1905 and is courtesy of the Arizona Historical Society.

Chapter Nine

When Fred Volz discovered the value of the Meteor Iron that was found in and around the great crater, he and his family gathered it and shipped it to buyers in the east. During the cutting process, the buyers of the meteoric iron discovered very tiny diamonds in the ore. For a long time this fact remained a closely guarded secret. Several strangers entered the rolling country looking around, hoping to find a diamond mine. Those contained in the iron were too small and too difficult of recovery to be profitable so they left very discouraged.

Below is a photo of Fred Volz and his wife that was taken circa 1900 and was found in our National Archives.

Unknown at this early stage of Meteor Crater's history was that not all the outer space visitor was composed of iron. There had also been in the mass a stony, slate-like substance. This material contained larger diamonds that could be broken out with a hammer.

A few years after the diamond hunters left the area a mysterious and elderly prospector by the name of Adolph Cannon, discovered the diamonds. The stony material was not identified for many years. Today this fact is denied, or that any diamonds whatever are found in meteorite fragments; but this is likely a safeguard to prevent a wild diamond hunting rush leading to a stampede of prospectors. Not all of the land over which the fragments fell on contact with the earth is under control to prevent pillage.

Cannon was a non-talking man who went to Winslow not more than three times a year for necessary supplies. During the winters he lived in the smaller caves of upper Canyon Diablo, but never in the Apache death cave. He always carried a large sum of currency when in town. Yet he never sold any diamonds. This transaction would have had to be made in or through a railroad town. That he had collected many pokes of diamonds is certain. Over the years he was seen picking up meteor fragments and breaking them out.

Sheepherders, cowboys and prospectors who spied on him occasionally, thought he searched for outlaws' stolen loot near Two Guns that was taken by the Canyon Diablo train robbers in 1889, who claimed they buried most of the stolen loot. He certainly hunted far from where it was supposedly buried. Reputable men observing Cannon over the years when they had business with him were convinced that he cached a hoard of diamonds. Also hidden away in caves and cliff dwellers' ruins were more pieces of the exploded meteorite picked up on the range.

For something like thirty years Cannon plodded the widely strewn area. At his heels followed a burro carrying panniers slung from a forked saddle. When finding a piece of meteorite, he knew contained one or more diamonds, he tossed it into a pannier.

Exaggerated tales spread about Cannon's hoard of diamonds. One individual meeting him unexpectedly in the area offered to make contacts for their sale. The yarns also drew hard cases who hoped to rob him of the alleged wealth in stones. On one occasion at least, two were prevented from killing him from ambush by a deer hunter who followed them until they assumed ambush positions. After driving them off, the hunter warned Cannon, who simply laughed but thanked the man for saving his life.

The old man, approaching eighty, was seen alive the last time in 1917. Then in 1928 a gravel hauler found the skeleton of a man in a pit east of Winslow on the Little Colorado. The skull had two bullet holes in it. Investigating lawmen found with the skeleton and rotted clothing a wallet containing a piece of paper with his name on it, a small mug shot of Cannon taken when a younger man and a pocket knife known to belong to him. From this evidence, clothing buttons, belt buckle and *"buck"* teeth, the remains were legally established as those of Cannon. The coroner's physician said that he had been dead at least ten years.

No money whatever was found with the skeleton, and no diamonds. The investigating officers theorized that robbery was the motive for his murder. But they could not account for how he happened to be on the river near Winslow so far from his regular stomping grounds.

Not long after discovery of his skeleton a burly man staggered into a Pitchfork line camp near Jack's Canyon. Fatally wounded, he had a buckskin pouch filled rough diamonds. Before dying he told the two cowboys stationed there that he and a partner had found one of Cannon's diamond caches, over which they had fought. After being wounded from a bushwhack position, shot the man then killed his partner, shooting him twice with a six-gun.

Although the cowboys tried to get him to the Winslow hospital the unknown man, nothing by way of identification on him, died at sunup while on the way to the hospital. The cowboys informed the local deputy sheriff of the matter, and hastened to Black's jewelry store where they showed the glistening white stones to the proprietor. Making tests, he pronounced them diamonds of a good industrial quality. Taking the next train to California the cowboys were not seen
again in Arizona.

The sheriff's deputy took a search party out hunting for the camp where the fatal fight supposedly had taken place. They could not find it nor did they find the body of a dead man.

The zoo was discontinued before Two Guns was sold to S. I. Richardson in 1950. For the next decade the property was leased to several operators, until purchased by Two

Guns Inc., Benjamin F. Dresher, general manager. Under his management new buildings have been constructed on Interstate 40 in keeping with western atmosphere and tradition.

Two Guns consists of a new motel, coffee shop and restaurant, gift and curio shop, western tavern and lounge and an up-to-date service station and garage. U. S. Postal facilities had been restored to the area and Justice Court has reopened for that precinct of Coconino County. Two Guns has also organized its own Chamber of Commerce with members throughout the entire county. Hench's zoo on the canyon wall was rebuilt, and a reptile exhibit has been added. All the old ruins of Cundiff's and Miller's stone buildings are being restored. Trails have been made through the old sites and guided tours are conducted daily.

While leveling off a car parking lot with a bulldozer before the Hopi house over the cave, several graves were cut into. Mrs. Hench does not recall any burials there during her time, unless Miller buried two or three Indians. However, the skull of at least one burial is that of a middle-aged white man.

The Apache death cave was explored between three and four miles underground at an early date. Miller inspected it underground in the belief that he might discover another Carlsbad Cavern.

The series of caverns never widen out or enlarge beyond the size of the first two. Two Winslow men explored them to an estimated seven and a half miles. Subsequently amateur speleologists reached that point, apparently at the end. However, a stone obstruction fallen from overhead was broken through into the next cavern. They then explored the series of caves for a distance of nine miles altogether.

In recent years a rock slide from the ceiling blocked entrance from the fifth cavern to the sixth, about 500 feet from the cave entrance. How were the caverns created? Two popular explanations are most often given. One is that when the great meteor struck it ruptured horizontal strata of stone, creating many cracks and fissures across the plateau. In several cases the overlying structures were not fractured.

The second theory, and one that holds considerable plausibility, is that they came into being during earth upheavals of the volcanic period which created the San Francisco Mountains. Many such open fissures are visible, north towards Cameron from U. S.

Highway 89. In appearance they resemble deep, black-colored arroyos.

Other great, open cracks in the earth's crust reach to the Little Colorado. Some contain water where Indian flocks can be trailed down to it. Blind fish have been found in these underground streams.

Two Guns, Arizona, still in existence, still a trading post, still located in one of the most historic and interesting areas of the great American Southwest, is one of those places where what went before meets with what is now. For the traveler, it is an oasis for rest and refreshment; for the historian, it is a symbol of the past; for everyone, it is of interest. Two Guns, Arizona, richly deserves its proud place on the map.

Below is a newspaper article that appeared in the Flagstaff Sun Newspaper on April 9, 2011. The mystery of Two Guns, still continues to this day.

Russell Crowe purchases Ghost town "Two Guns" in Arizona

By Frank DiAmmato on April 9, 2011

Would you like to own your own Ghosttown? Got 3 Million dollars to Spend and it is yours!.

Russell Crowe has been trying to start production on the film West World for over 12 years now Russell loves westerns and rumor has it that this film is now on the front burner with producer Jerry Weintraub at the helm. But the original film released in 1973 was written by Michael Crichton Dubbed "The Father of the Techno Thriller," and Michael who owns the rights to the film also wants to produce West World Part 2 in 2013.

Russell's solution, simply change the name, now called "Two Guns"; the film is about two guests at a high-tech amusement park who go on a Wild West adventure. The park is peopled by robots and is designed to provide a 100% life like experience simulating Roman times, cowboy times, and medieval times. When the park's central computer breaks down, the robots start to run amok and our two guests find themselves stalked by a robot gunslinger.

Russell was originally planning to film the movie in Sydney Australia so he could stay close to home, however when a friend told him about a Ghost Town that was for sale and on the market in Arizona, Russell decided to have a look himself.

Two Guns is a real Ghost Town located in Arizona close to Interstate

40. The original owner has been trying to sell it for several years, with a price tag of 3 million, no electric, broken gas pumps, and empty zoo cages and dilapidating ruins, it was not the ideal investment.

However, when both producer Jerry Weintraub and Crowe looked at the property, it would also include a portion of some other property know as Canyon Diablo. Canyon Diablo is known as "The worst trail town in Arizona-perhaps the entire West"..."the toughest Hellhole in the West"... and "the West's most deadly town." Between 1880 and 1882, there were more killings as a result of gunfights, robberies, and murders took place there than in Tombstone, Dodge City, and Abilene, Kansas combined.

If Tombstone was noted for "having a man for breakfast every morning," then it could be said that Canyon Diablo "had a man for breakfast, lunch, and supper every day." The history of Two Guns and Canyon Diablo was just what the film; now called Two Guns needed, some realistic, futuristic and historic embellishments to be included into the story's theme.

For now, Two Guns is closed with a sign on the gate No Trespassers, but in the near future this Ghost

Town will turn into a nightmare of tractor trailers and production crews. Maybe when Crowe is done he will convert it into his living space, Crowe's Hellhole in the West.

Below is a photo of what remains of the ghost town of Two Guns which is located thirty miles east of Flagstaff on the south side of Interstate forty. It is almost directly across I-40 from the Navajo Casino of Twin Arrows. This photo was taken by the author's friend Mike Rupp.

Chapter Ten

While completing the research this book the author came across the work of the late Gladwell Richardson an amazing prolific historian and writer, who without his research and personal interviews, this book would never have been completed. Richardson lived among the Navajo people, and was able to build a close relationship with them, allowing him to interview them and they opened up to him sharing their stories.

Toney Gladwell Richardson is a relatively unknown to we Arizonians but was a prolific author, who spent more than twenty years living and working on the Navajo Reservation in northern Arizona. He was drawn to the Native American's that lived in Northern Arizonan. Being part Native American himself he spent a lot of time researching their culture and wrote over three hundred books relating directly the Navajo people in Arizona.

Gladwell Richardson's newspaper articles and interviews of the three Navajo Chiefs involved in this story were of great value as I researched and wrote this story. Native American's are generally not willing to share their history but since Richardson was part Native American that lived and worked amongst them, they were willing share their history with him. The Navajo people are very traditional and the Native American population in general did not keep good historical records. Information about their history was told to a chosen few from generation to generation.

Gladwell Richardson was born September 4, 1903 in Alverado Texas to Susan Meador Richardson and her husband S.I. Richardson. Gladwell, or *"Toney"* as he was known to his friends had two siblings, a brother named Cecil, who also became an author and served as sheriff of Coconino County Arizona for a number of years, and a younger sister, Irbymae who was born in 1910. In 1910, the family moved to Kitty Oklahoma, a town a couple of miles north-west of present day Clarita which is now abandoned. With the exception of a short time spent in Winslow Arizona, he and his family lived in Kitty and Clarita Oklahoma for the next eight years. Much of the material later found in Richardson's writing came from his experiences during this important time of his life.

Encouraged by his father to wear western attire and learn to rope and ride, Gladwell got to know both the cowboys who worked the numerous cattle operations in the area and many of the Choctaw and Chickasaw tribal members that resided around Clarita and Olney. He made many life-long friends with whom he communicated until his death in 1980. Among the long-time residents of the area who knew him and with whom he exchanged correspondence or tried to stay in touch, were Mrs. Winston P. (Billie) Rice, George MacMillan, Ernest Riley, Lee Gentry Elliston and George Allen.

In 1914, S.I. Richardson bought a six-room hotel in Clarita and moved his family there. It was at this time that young Gladwell joined the "Lone Scouts," an organization similar to today's Boy Scouts which emphasized. He was rewarded by gathering of scientific information which was then distributed to other "Lone Scout" chapters throughout the nation. Gladwell specialized in collecting fossils which he displayed in an empty upstairs room of his father's hotel. This *"self-education"* was supplemented by attendance at the Clarita public school where he remembered passing notes to Beatrice O'Neal while in high school. In September of 1919, he enrolled at Oklahoma Agricultural and Mechanical College (OSU) where he did well (B+ average) but he chose not to return after the first year.

His formal education over, Gladwell spent time in Arizona working in Navajo trading posts before joining the military sometime in 1920. His first chose the Marines, but when it was discovered that he was underage, the chaplain (at his father's request) got him discharged. He immediately re-enlisted in the Navy, where he served for over fifty years as an active-duty seaman or in the reserves. While on active duty he traveled extensively, visiting Guam, Japan and Russia before his discharge from active service in 1924. He was recalled after Pearl Harbor and served in the South Pacific. It was here that he ran in to some of his old friends from his trading post days, the famous Navajo Code Talkers. After World War II, he continued in the reserves until he was once again recalled to active duty for the Korean War where he served as chief journalist until he was finally discharged once again from the regular navy. He continued to serve in the reserves until a 1973 stroke finally ended his military career.

Richardson's career as a writer began in 1924 as soon as he was discharged from his first tour of active duty. He briefly returned to Arizona where he supported himself by working in an Indian curio store owned by relatives before moving to Modesto California to help nurse his ill brother Cecil. It was here that he met his future wife, Millicent Margaret Green. They were Married in June of 1925 and lived together fifty-five years. The couple produced two daughters, Cecile, born March 1, 1926 and Toni born January 9, 1939. The young couple supported themselves first by working at a cannery in Modesto and then driving to Arizona where they helped out working in family owned trading posts on the Navajo reservation.

The fall of 1928 found them at Inscription House Trading Post which had been recently established by Gladwell's father. They worked during the day waiting on customers and improving the trading post's meager facilities, but in the evening and on weekends, Gladwell and Millie worked as a writing team. "Toney" composed while Millie edited and typed. Gladwell also began establishing the network of contacts necessary for success as a professional writer. Besides getting to know other writers, he obtained the services of Robert Hardy as his agent. Hardy succeeded in selling many of Toney's magazine articles, but was unable to sell his full-length novels to American publishing houses. He was, however, able to get the attention of the English publisher Curtiss Brown Limited and later another English firm, Ward Locke.

Gladwell and Millie churned out hundreds of novels which Hardy sold for from $250.00 to $350.00 per book. Although all of them were published in England Richardson also succeeded in selling the American rights to magazines such as Complete Western who published his books in serial form. Another big break came in 1932 when a Hollywood movie company purchased the film rights to his novel, Gun Puncher for $150.00.

Working at various trading posts, writing and finally directing the Flagstaff Pow-Wow got Gladwell and Millie through the 1920's and the Great Depression. The Flagstaff Pow-Wow became one of the United States most famous western celebrations under his stewardship. By 1936, over seven thousand Native Americans attended. Tribes from throughout North America were represented, including the Kiowa, Cherokee and Choctaw tribes of Oklahoma. In 1937, Richardson convinced a major New York radio station to give play-by-play coverage to the event. At Inscription House Trading Post, Gladwell served as a guide for tourists interested in seeing the Anasazi ruins located nearby. This job allowed him to make several important contacts in the literary world, including Randall Henderson, the editor and publisher of The Desert Magazine, who soon became a major buyer of his stories.

The interruption of World War II and the Korean Conflict broke up the writing team of Gladwell and Millie, and they did not get back on track until the late 1950's. Western Novels were not selling like they once were, so it was at this point that Gladwell began the last phase of his literary career when he started to concentrate almost exclusively on magazine articles. By the late 1960's and early 1970's most of Richardson's articles appeared in western and treasure magazine's like True West, Frontier Times, Old West and Zane Gray Western Magazine. My grandfather, Ernest Riley, introduced me to Richardson's work in 1971 when he showed me an article in True West Magazine that described events around Clarita.

The author of the article was listed as Maurice Kildare, one of several pen names employed by Richardson over the course of his career. Besides Maurice Kildare, Richardson's pen names included John R. Winslowe, Calico Jones, Warren O'Riley, Robert Hart Davis, Carey James, George Blacksnake Ormond Clarkson, Cary James, Frank Warner, Grant Maxwell, Buck Coleman and Robert Hart. One reason Gladwell used pen names was because it allowed him to publish more than one story in a single edition of a magazine. A single issue of Zane Gray Western Magazine from 1971 to 1975 might have as many as five Gladwell Richardson stories; all under different pen names.

As Gladwell Richardson's literary career neared its end his thoughts turned more and more to the formative days of his youth. He had a burning desire to revisit the haunts of his high school days and visit with his childhood friends. In the early 1970's he heard that a Clarita reunion was planned and expressed a desire to attend. He contacted Billie Rice to obtain information on the event and they soon became frequent correspondents. In 1973, however, as he was making final plans for the trip back to Oklahoma, he suffered a debilitating stroke that forced its cancellation. He recovered partially, but was soon hobbled further by diabetes. Finally, in 1981, Gladwell Richardson contracted cancer and died.

The career of Gladwell "Toney" Richardson was an amazing one. He is estimated to have published more than three hundred novels and perhaps as many as five thousand magazine articles and short stories. His novels, all published in England, were translated from English into Spanish, Polish, Dutch, Czechoslovakian, Spanish, and Scandinavian. It is further estimated that, in all, he published about sixty million words in his lifetime. Although he has been dead for over twenty-five years, there is still a strong demand for his work.

Acknowledgments

Tales of the Little Colorado,
   By Joe Jeffers and Apache Indian, the by Frank C. Lockwood. The Macmillan Company, New York, N.Y, 1938

Adventures in the Apache Country,
   By I. Ross, Browne, Harper and Brothers Publishing, New York, N.Y.. 1869.

Arizona Characters,
   By F. C. Lockwood, Los Angeles Times Mirror Press, Los Angeles, California, 1928.

Arizona Place Names,
   By Will C. Barnes, University of Arizona Press, Tucson, Arizona, 1935.

A Reconnaissance of Parts of North Western Arizona, by N.H. Darton, USGS. Bulletin 435, 1854.

Alluring Arizona,
   By W. H. Nelson. Privately Published in 1927.

Arizona and its Heritage,

Journalism school publication, University of Arizona Press, Tucson, Arizona, 1936

An Ethnological Dictionary. The Franciscan Missionary Fathers, St. Michaels Mission, Arizona, 1910.

Chronologic List of Engagements of the Indian Wars, the United States Army, National Archives, 1929

Days in the Painted Desert,
    By H. S. Colton, Museum of Northern Arizona, Flagstaff, Arizona, 1932.

Expedition into New Mexico,
    Recorded by Antonio de Espejo in 1582, Published by Diego P. Lujan, University of New Mexico Press, Albuquerque, N.M., 1940

Expedition of de Vargas, into New Mexico,
    By J. Manuel Espinosa, University of New Mexico Press, Albuquerque N.M., 1940

Geology of the Navajo Country,
    By H. E. Gregory. U.S. Water Supply Paper, No.380, the United

States Government Printing Office, Document number 916

The Great American Plateau,
   by T. M. Prudden. Putnam and
   Co. Publishing, New York, N.Y.,
   1907.

History of Arizona, By Thomas E. Farish,
   Filmer Brothers Publishing, San Francisco, CA. in 1915

History of Arizona, by James H.
   McClintock. S. J. Clarke Company Publishing, Chicago, IL, 1976

History of New Mexico and Arizona,
   by H. H. Bancroft, The Bancroft Co Publishing, New York, N.Y., 1888

Indian Claims Commssion Report, Dockets
   No. 1 through Docket 229, the Navajo Tribe, Window Rock, Arizona, 1966

Indians of the Painted Desert,
   By Leo Crane, Little Brown Publishing Company, New York, N.Y., 1925

Indian Blankets and Their Makers,
 By George W. lames, A.C. McClurg & Company, Chicago, IL, 1927.

The Journey of Coronado,
 By George P. Winthrop, A. S. Barnes & Company Publishing, New York, N.Y., 1904

Mesa Land,
 By Anna W. Ickes. Houghton Mifflin Co., New York, N.Y., 1933

Mesa, Canon and Pueblo,
 By Charles F. Lummis. The Century Company Publishing, New York, N.Y., 1925

Missions and Pueblos of the Old Southwest, by Earle B. Forrest, A. H. Clarke Co., Chicago, IL. 1929

Mormon Settlement in Arizona,
 By I. H. McClintock, University of Arizona Press, Tucson, Arizona, 1921

Navajo Trading Days,
 By Elizabeth Compton Hegemann. University of New Mexico Press, 1963

New Mexico, American Guide Series,
   Hastings House Publishing, New
   York, N.Y., 1940

Navajo Bibliography,
   By A.I. Lee Correll and Edith L.
   Watson, The Navajo Tribe
   Publishing, Window Rock, Arizona
   1967

Navajo Weaving,
   By C. A. Amsden, Fine Arts Press
   Santa Ana, California, 1934

Navajo Indians,
   By Dane & Mary R. Coolidge.
   Houghton, Mifflin Company Press,
   New York, N.Y., 1930

Navajo Legends,
   By George W. Matthews. American
   Folklore Society Publishing, New
   York, N.Y., 1897.

Navajo Country,
   By Herbert F. Gregory, U.S
   Government Printing Office,
   Washington, D.C., 1916

On The Border with Crook,
   Written by John G. Bourke, Charles
   Scribners & Sons Publishing, New

York, N.Y., 1892

Old Bill Williams, Mountain Man,
   By A. H. Favour, University of North Carolina Press, Chapel Hill, N.C., 1936

Old Trails West,
   By Ralph Moody, Thomas Y. Crowell Company Publishing, New York, N.Y., 1963

On the Trail of a Spanish Pioneer,
   by Elliot Coucs. The University of Arizona Press, Tucson, AZ., 1900

Personal Narrative of James O Pattie,
   by Pattie Donnelly, Anderson & Sons Publishing, Chicago, IL, 1930

Pioneer Days in Arizona,
   by F. C. Lockwood, The Macmillian Company Publishing, New York, N.Y., 1932

Report on a Wagon Road between Fort Defiance and the Colorado River,
   by Edward F. Beale, U.S. Senate Exchange Document, Serial Number 959

Report on a Wagon Road from Fort Smith,
    Arkansas to the Colorado River, Edward F. Beale, United States House of Representatives, Document Volume 6, Published in 1890.

Report on the Colorado River of the West,
    By J. C. Ives, United States Senate, Document Number 90, 1860.

Report on an Expedition, the Zuni and Colorado Rivers, by Lt. Lorenzo Sitgreaves, Senate Document LX, Number 59, published in 1853

Report on the Explorations for building a Railroad Route,
    by A. W. Whipple, U.S. Senate Document 760 and 761, 1855

Santa Fe, the Railroad That Built an Empire,
    By James Marshall, Random House Publishing, New York, NY, 1945

Wrangling the Past,
    By Frank M. King. Privately

Published, Los Angeles, CA, 1935

Vanished Arizona,
 By Martha Summerhays, The Salem Press, Salem. MA, 1911

Apache Death Cave,
 By Maurice Kildare, Big West Publishing Company, Los Angeles, CA. 1967

Arizona's Mystery Cave,
 By Gladwell Richardson, Arizona Highways Magazine, Phoenix, Arizona, Published on Dec. 3, 1967

Dynasty of Indian Traders,
 By Maurice Kildare, Western Publications, Austin TX, 1968

The Devils Canyon,
 By John R. Winslowe, Big West Publishing, Los Angeles, CA 1950

The Dead Must Drink,
 By Gladwell Richardson, Arizona Highways Magazine, June, 1963

Care for the Dead,
 By Maurice Kildare, Desert Magazine, Tucson, Arizona, September, 1967

History of the Cattle Industry in Arizona,
   By Bert Haskett, Arizona Historical
   Review, October, 1936

History of the Sheep Industry in Arizona,
   By Bert Haskett, Arizona Historical
   Review, July, 1936

Keno Harry,
   By Maurice Kildare, Real West
   Magazine, Los Angeles, California,
   January, 1967

Lost Meteor Diamonds,
   By Maurice Kildare, Old West
   Magazine, Santa Fe, NM, Fall 1967

Meteor Crater,
   By H. N. Russell. Museum of
   Northern Arizona, Vol.4, Number 3,
   Flagstaff, Arizona, 1931

The Meteor Crater Story,
   by George Foster. Meteor Crater
   Enterprises, Inc., Flagstaff,
   Arizona, 1964

Meteor Mountain,
   By Pauline Claffey, Arizona
   Highways, Magazine, Phoenix,
   Arizona, September, 1938

The Most Interesting Spot on Earth,
 By Vera F. Sliter, People Magazine of Arizona, Phoenix AZ October, 1939.

Old Wolf Trading Post, by Gladwell Richardson, the Coconino Sun Newspaper, Flagstaff, AZ., 1939

Stone Artifacts of the San Francisco Mountain Region,
 By Katharine Bartlett, Museum of Northern Arizona, Vol.3, No.6, Flagstaff, Arizona, 1930.

Canyon Diablo,
 By Zeke Crandall, Zeke Crandall Publishing LLC, Glendale, AZ, ISBN Number 978-09773784-6-3

Ghost in the Desert,
 By Zeke Crandall, Zeke Crandall Publishing LLC, Glendale, AZ. ISBN Number 978-09773784-1-8

Pleasant Valley Revisited,
 By Zeke Crandall, Zeke Crandall Publishing LLC, Glendale AZ, ISBN Number 978-09773784-7-0

Wikipedia Online Encyclopedia, by
 By Jim Wales, with various articles

and contributors, Wikimedia Foundation, One Montgomery St., #1600, San Francisco CA, 94104

About the Author

William "Tom" Vyles aka Zeke Crandall was born in London, Ontario, Canada. The family moved to Phoenix, Arizona in 1956. A life long battle with Asthma, several bouts with pneumonia, in an out of hospitals the first nine years of life, the family was instructed by physicians to move to Arizona for the hot dry climate.

In and out of school until age ten, home schooled by his mother Elizabeth, reading "The Books of Knowledge," encyclopedia, Tom fell in love with history. With no family in Arizona, our family adopted elderly neighbors, Kenny and Mary Harris, as our Arizona grandparents.

Kenny worked in the stockyards in Cincinnati as a brand inspector for cattle coming from Arizona. He became friends of John Wayne, who brought his cattle through the stockyards in Cincinnati. John talked Kenny into moving to Arizona. Kenny was a professional fiddle player, along with his friend Rudy MacDonald, who played banjo, they toured Arizona playing gigs.

Young Tom went along on most of the out of town music gigs. His job was to set up instruments and equipment. The carrot for Tom was that Kenny would take me rabbit and quail hunting the next day. Young Tom fell in love with Arizona history, because Kenny introduced him to many amazing older men, who told him stories of the old west.

www.ingramcontent.com/pod-product-compliance
Lightning Source LLC
Chambersburg PA
CBHW062226080426
42734CB00010B/2042